Points of Interest walks in and around West Yorkshire

Roy Ellwood

2016

Copyright © 2016 by Roy Ellwood

All rights reserved. This book or any portion thereof may not be reproduced or used in any manner whatsoever without the express written permission of the publisher except for the use of brief quotations in a book review or scholarly journal.

First Printing 2016

ISBN 978-1-326-79612-9

Contents

Introduction	1
POI1 – The Wainhouse Walk, Halifax	3
POI2 – The Skipton Walk	15
POI3 – The Ilkley Walk	31
POI4 – The Hebden Bridge Walk	47
POI5 – The Haworth Walk	63
POI6 – The Saltaire Walk	81
POI7 – The Holmfirth Walk	97
POI8 – The Harrogate Walk	109
POI9 – The Knaresborough Walk	127
POI10 – The Otley Walk	145

Introduction

This book contains details of 10 short walks in towns in, or near, West Yorkshire.

Each walk is on hard surfaces and should not necessitate the wearing of boots or special clothing.

Along the way the walk shows you all the Points of Interest in the town.

For every walk there is an accompanying 'app' for Android powered devices, available in Google Play Store, for you to download free, so that you make take a smartphone or tablet with you whilst on the walk as an alternative to taking this book.

To download from Play Store it is recommended to enter the name of the walk into their search facility rather than the walk ID – eg enter 'Hebden Bridge' instead of POI4.

Additional copies of this book can be ordered online from www.lulu.com

Points of Interest walks in and around West Yorkshire

POI1 – Halifax, The Wainhouse Walk

The walk is an easy stroll around the area of Halifax where John Edward Wainhouse lived and worked, on the hillside from Savile Park towards Sowerby Bridge.

It is approximately 2 miles but can take up to 1.5 hours because of all the points of interest to view en route.

Underfoot is virtually all tarmac or cobbles so hopefully muddy feet can be avoided. Unfortunately, the walk has some steep slopes and is not recommended for wheelchairs.

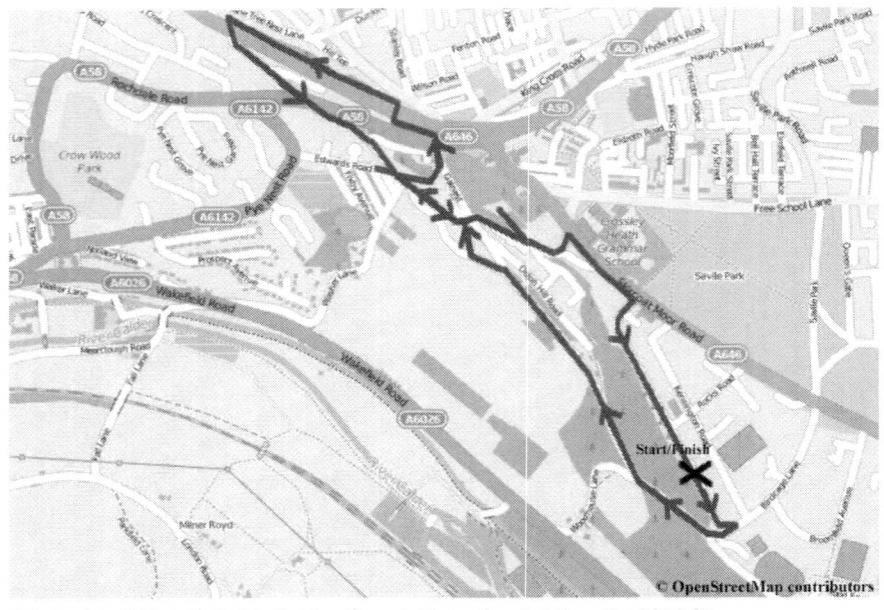

This data is available under the Open Database license and the cartography is licensed as CC BY-SA
Visit http://www.openstreetmap.org/copyright and opendatacommons.org for full copyright details

POI1 - The Wainhouse Walk, Halifax

START: Lower section of Albert Promenade, Halifax, HX3 0HZ.

There is plenty of parking and no yellow lines. You cannot drive the whole length of Albert Promenade as a barrier has been placed half way and, although it is tempting to walk up this magnificent promenade and take in the view, at the end of the walk we take in the full length of this road from top to bottom.

Right now, we must return to the junction with Birdcage Lane and turn right down the hill into Birdcage Hill.

Half way down Birdcage Hill, turn right into Scarr Bottom Road.

After about 800 yards, we come across a row of what were originally Almshouses, but now privately owned, and our first encounter with John Edward Wainhouse.

You will obviously also see above the cottages the huge edifice of Wainhouse Tower, which we will meet close up later on the walk. In the 1870s, Wainhouse added the lower 3 cottages to the original 5 and added porches to all 8.

Originally, these cottages all had interconnecting doors so you could go from one to another without having to go outside.

Points of Interest walks in and around West Yorkshire

Immediately opposite the cottages turn left into a small lane going down the hill - Master Lane (unsigned at this end). You will pass a building on the left named Sapling Cottage. You soon come across a junction of 3 lanes and gates with the nameplates of Sapling Dene and Sapling Dell.

This is private property and not to be entered, and is now 3 dwellings as at the rear of the property is another gateway leading to the current Sapling Grove.

When it was a single dwelling, the entire mansion was called Sapling Grove and was the residence of Wainhouse's uncle Robert, who owned a large Dye house (now a small industrial estate) just below the mansion and further west.

Wainhouse (and his two sisters) moved here to live with their uncle when their mother died in 1829 when Wainhouse was just 12 years old. Sapling Grove today is just half of the original mansion and cannot be seen on our walk.

It is not known what role, if any, Wainhouse had with his uncle's Dye house, but he inherited the entire works and many more properties locally in 1856, aged 39, when his uncle passed away.

His sisters also benefited from the death of their uncle, but Wainhouse bought their shares of works and property for £20,000 each. What we do know is that he let the Works Manager, Henry Mossman, run the company and had little to do with it himself.

Later, in 1870, he leased the works to Mossman, finally selling it to him in 1873, and Mossman moved into Sapling Grove as that was part of the sale too.

POI1 - The Wainhouse Walk, Halifax

From the gates of Sapling Dene walk up the hill opposite to reach another junction where we turn left along Upper Washer Lane.

Upon selling the dye works, Wainhouse had a new house built - West Air - now the Wainhouse Tavern.

Continue along Upper Washer Lane and you will see it on the right. He didn't move here immediately upon vacating Sapling Grove but lived for a while at another house, now 37-39 Delph Hill Terrace, Halifax, HX2 7EJ, but then called Delville.

West Air has many unusual features Including two mottos carved into the stonework; "Crede Coleri" = "Believe in Colour" (reference to dye working) and "Parcere subjectis et deballere superbos" = "Spare the lowly and make war on the proud" (rumoured to be reference to his dislike and feud with Sir Henry Edwards, his next-door neighbour). Notice that at West Air no two windows that are alike. Wainhouse died here, unmarried, in 1883 aged 66.

From West Air walk a few yards down Edwards Road to the bus stop on the right and within the wall, you will see a stone-carved plaque with the initials of John Edward Wainhouse. Wainhouse would turn in his grave if he knew about this as it was repositioned here when an outbuilding of West Air was demolished. It now sits within the estate of his archenemy Sir Henry Edwards (hence Edwards Road).

It is odd that Wainhouse built his new house right next to the boundary of the two estates. He and Edwards rowed over wells and watercourses that ran through their estates and all over this hillside. Wainhouse even had a number of pamphlets published and distributed at his own expense lampooning Edwards.

Points of Interest walks in and around West Yorkshire

Back to West Air and to the left of the pub is Stoney Lane (well named) which is a very (very) steep cobbled pathwhich we must climb - SLOWLY !!!!

At the top, turn left and walk uphill over the cobbles. At the top of this short stretch you climb to Rochdale Road - use the steps on the right.

When you arrive at Rochdale Road, you will see across the road the once magnificent Wainhouse Terrace.

Cross the road at this point and climb the first flight of about 10 steps opposite and then go left on Burnley Road.

The terrace is now overgrown and dangerous so do not explore it too much. Along the top once stood a terrace of houses owned by Wainhouse to which he added balconies and this current structure below the houses.

POI1 - The Wainhouse Walk, Halifax

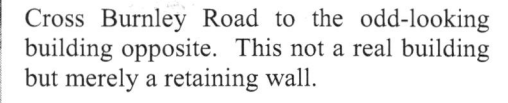

Cross Burnley Road to the odd-looking building opposite. This not a real building but merely a retaining wall.

Once a farmstead stood here called the Allan Fold and when it was demolished to widen the road, the builders used its front wall to construct this peculiar retaining wall as a 'ghost' of the building itself.

The original Allan Fold farm.

Walk along Burnley Road until you come across a set of steps leading up the hillside.

Climb one set of the steps and look up and you will see a stone carved with the initials of John Edward Wainhouse - now down the other set of steps and back to Burnley Road.

Points of Interest walks in and around West Yorkshire

About half a mile further along Burnley Road cross the main road again and descend Green Lane.

At the bottom of Green Lane cross the busy Rochdale Road once again and descend further down Darcey Hey Lane, back to the Wainhouse Tavern and retrace your steps along Upper Washer Lane.

This time, just past West Air, look to your left and you will see a well, built at his own cost by Wainhouse, with his initials above.

Continue along Upper Washer Lane to return to an earlier junction with Wakefield Gate, which we must now climb.

Half way up Wakefield Gate, turn sharp left along a track leading to the Tower.

POI1 - The Wainhouse Walk, Halifax

Finally, we reach the tower.

Begun in 1871, it was for use by the dye works, 350 metres further down the hillside, with a planned underground tunnel to take smoke away from the valley.

Its construction (a common solution in its day) was forced to some degree, as many factories were then being prosecuted under the new Smoke Abatement Act.

In 1874, when Wainhouse sold the dye works to Henry Mossman, Henry Mossman declined to buy the then nearly completed chimney as he didn't want responsibility for it.

It is commonly thought that the chimney was abandoned for use as such and then clad in stone with the inclusion of a spiral staircase to the top (403 steps), but this is not true as it was always planned and built to have this stone cladding and the staircase.

Complaints persisted against Henry Mossman for smoke pollution (from Sir Henry Edwards for one) but he successfully defended a prosecution by installing fans and building a new chimney on the dye works' premises without the need to make use of the Tower chimney.

The elaborate top was redesigned and, being accessible by the staircase, is sometimes referred to as the Observatory. There is a local tale told that Wainhouse did this out of spite to be able to look into the estate of his hated neighbour Sir Henry Edwards, who had built a wall around to stop people doing just that. There may be some truth here? Notice that, as at West Air, all the windows in the tower are of different designs.

Points of Interest walks in and around West Yorkshire

On the lower side of the base is a blocked up archway, which was intended for the flue to enter.

The tower is 253 feet high, eight sided, and was finished on 9 September 1875 requiring 9000 tons of stone to construct at a cost of about £14000 when wages were £1 per week.

The inner chimney is simply made of brick. Very little mortar was used in the construction as Wainhouse preferred a dowelling technique with copper pins, as in all his other buildings such as West Air.

Following the death of Wainhouse, it had a number of private owners until the local council acquired it following a public subscription, on 30 May 1919.

The Tower is open for the public to ascend, for a small charge, on Bank holidays and selected dates through the year - contact Calderdale council or Visitor Information Centre for details.

Wainhouse, himself, used to allow local clubs and churches to use the tower for a day or so in order that they profit from allowing visitors to ascend.

Leaving the Tower, we head to Skircoat Moor Road. There are 3 ways to get there from the Tower, two dirt-like paths leading from the grassy area at the foot of the tower (both of which can be very muddy after rain) or the recommendation is to retrace your steps to Wakefield Gate and continue up the steep cobbled road.

POI1 - The Wainhouse Walk, Halifax

Once at Skircoat Moor Rd (A646) turn right down the hill and on your left you will see Crossley Heath School - formed by the amalgamation of Crossley and Porter School and Heath Grammar School in 1986.

Originally, this was an 'Orphan Home and School for Boys and Girls' opened in 1864, thanks to the generosity of 3 brothers: Francis, John and Joseph Crossley.

In 1887, Thomas Porter made a donation to the orphanage on condition that his name be added to its name.

There are 12 cottages plus an assembly hall and a Matron's cottage, built by Harold Vincent Mackintosh and the Mackintosh family (of toffee fame, who are local to Halifax) and opened on 1st January 1925.

The homes were for married couples aged over 60, and ex-employees of Mackintosh, and members of the congregation of Queens Road United Methodist Church, who had a joint income of between £1 and £2 per week.

Today residents must still be over 60 and be local residents, but now there is no stipulation of income or of being an ex-employee.

Points of Interest walks in and around West Yorkshire

The local council acquired the land in 1866 from Henry Savile and the Savile family for £100, to be set apart as a recreation ground and to be called the Savile Park.

The council planned to turn it into a park. However, the council still didn't have control over the land as the Skircoat Board of Surveyors held 'rights' over the land although they didn't own it.

Our John Edward Wainhouse was not only a member of the Board but performed the negotiations with the council to sell their 'rights'. He asked for £12,000 which was an absurd amount - they offered £200 - and he eventually settled for £201 but with an agreement that no park be built and that it be left unenclosed in perpetuity.

We now return to Albert Promenade, with its magnificent views of the Ryburn valley and the Norland township and moor opposite.

There are number of benches to sit and enjoy the view and a last glimpse of Wainhouse Tower.

Albert Promenade was built by Henry Charles McCrea to allow Halifax residents to enjoy the view and The Rocks below (a recreational area of woodland) and opened in 1861.

I hope that you enjoyed the walk.

POI1 - The Wainhouse Walk, Halifax

Points of Interest walks in and around West Yorkshire

POI2 – The Skipton Walk

The walk is an easy stroll around Skipton town centre.

It is approximately 2 miles but can take up to 1.5 hours because of all the points of interest to view en route.

It is mainly on hard surfaces.

Unfortunately, the walk has some steps and slopes and is not recommended for wheelchairs.

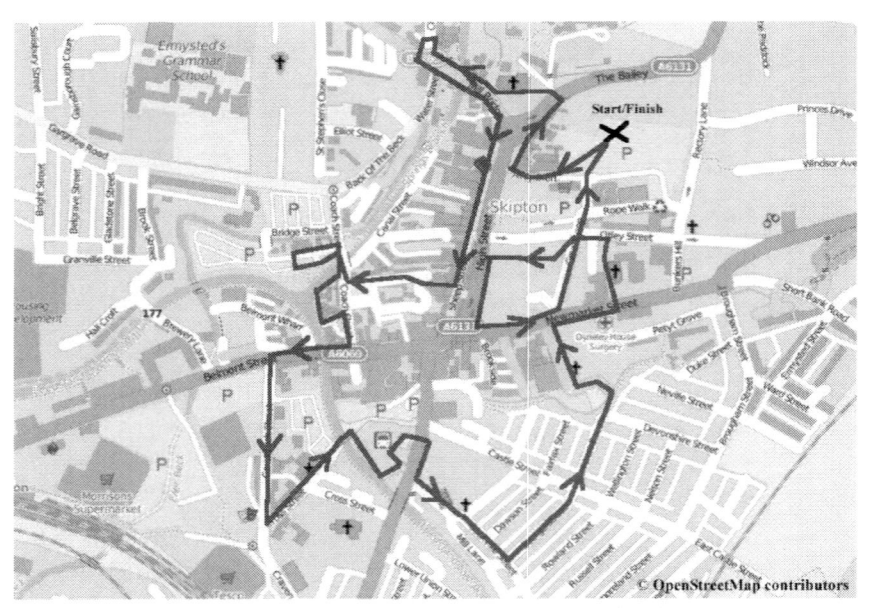

This data is available under the Open Database license and the cartography is licensed as CC BY-SA
Visit http://www.openstreetmap.org/copyright and opendatacommons.org for full copyright details

POI2 – The Skipton Walk

START: The walk starts in one of main town centre car parks, in the heart of Skipton, behind the Town Hall. Set your sat nav to BD23 1ED. (This is a Pay and Display car park.)

Leave the car park along this street, called Jerry Croft, towards the High Street, where if your visit is on a Monday, Wednesday, Friday or Saturday the market should be in full swing.

Turn to your right and you will be outside the current Town Hall.

You could visit the Town Hall, either now or at the end of the walk, as it contains the Tourist Information Office, toilets, the 'Craven Museum and Gallery' and a Collectors Craft and Gift Fair (on market days) plus a cafe too, all free entry, so well worth a visit.

On the outside of the Town Hall, there is a plaque to Herbert Smith 1889-1977.

He is acknowledged as the designer of all of Sopwith's fighting aircraft, such as the Camel, Triplane and Snipe used by the Royal Flying Corps during the First World War.

Points of Interest walks in and around West Yorkshire

You may notice two flagged paths amongst the cobbles outside the Town Hall, one crossing the road at right angles, the other at an angle towards the Church. This latter path is supposed to have been laid to protect the vicar's flowing cassocks from the muck of the cattle market as he made his way from the vicarage to the church and originally ran across what is today the tarmac of the road.

Keep walking up the hill with the War Memorial to your left keeping right at the roundabout in order to get a view of the entrance of the Castle.

The Castle is the biggest tourist attraction in Skipton and a tour is a must for visitors, but on this walk we merely get a view of the entrance gateway.

The original castle dates back as far as 1090 but has been rebuilt and modified numerous times and is now one of the most complete and best preserved castles in England

What you are viewing is the Gateway added in the 17th Century and is decorative rather than defensive. The motto over the gate is that of the Earls of Clifford who owned it - DES OR MAIS - 'Henceforth'.

POI2 – The Skipton Walk

Cross the road and pass across the front of the Holy Trinity Church.

The clock in the tower was installed in 1899 and is still working.

Originally a wooden structure built about 1090, the current stone church was begun around 1300.

Closely connected with the Clifford family, who owned the Castle, five Earls of Cumberland and three Countesses are buried inside.

Exit the High Street towards Mill Bridge across the Eller Beck, which joins the canal just below the bridge, and as you cross the bridge you will see the High Corn Mill to your right.

Go a little further along the road to the road junction and turn to your right.

You are about to visit the mill, which is free entry.

Walk a few yards up Chapel Hill and to the main entrance to the mill.

There was a corn mill recorded here in 1310.

The current building dates from the 18th century and until the 19th century all corn in the town had to be ground here, with a toll paid to the owner of the castle.

Points of Interest walks in and around West Yorkshire

Inside the mill, you will find a waterwheel that still works today.

Normally, it is stationary, but you can pull a handle in the ceiling to release water to make it turn.

Today the building also houses some offices and shops for you to browse.

Leave the Corn Mill and immediately opposite you should see the Wright Wine Company and here there is a plaque to record that John Wesley preached on this spot.

At the rear of this building, to the right, once stood the old pinfold, where stray sheep were impounded until their owners claimed them upon payment of a fine.

On the other side of the main road is the Royal Oak pub and beside it there is a cobbled road that used to lead down to a ford to cross the beck.

The bridge that now replaces it was built in 1628.

POI2 – The Skipton Walk

Now retrace your steps back across the bridge towards Holy Trinity church, and down the right hand side of the High Street.

Note the date stone on the wall of the Black Horse of 1676, but the inn itself dates back to the 15th Century (although not the oldest pub in Skipton, that honour being held by the Red Lion on the opposite side of the High Street, supposedly 1209 being the first record).

Also, outside the Black Horse is a set of stone steps to assist you to mount your horse.

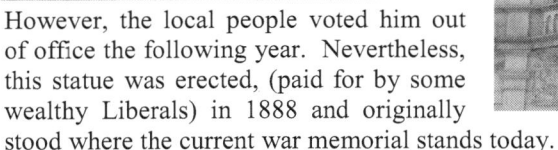

A little further down the High Street, outside the Free Library (another building worthy of note for its architecture) is the statue of Sir Mathew Wilson. He was Skipton's first MP after it had become its own constituency (1885) and was Liberal. However, the local people voted him out of office the following year. Nevertheless, this statue was erected, (paid for by some wealthy Liberals) in 1888 and originally stood where the current war memorial stands today.

Points of Interest walks in and around West Yorkshire

As you pass the current Yorkshire Bank glance at the plaque providing some history of the building. It was once the Bay Horse Inn where the Bull Baiting Stone stood in its forecourt.

During bull-baiting, trained dogs would attempt to flatten themselves to the ground, creeping as close to the bull as possible, then darting out and attempting to bite the bull in the nose or head area. The bull would be tethered by a collar and rope, which was staked into the ground. As a dog darted at the bull, the bull would attempt to catch the dog with his head and horns and throw it into the air.

A little further down the High Street you will see a Ginnel called Sterlings Yard, one of many off the High Street.

They lead to rows of small cottages crammed into the town as the only solution to a need for houses, as the owners of the land around the town (The Earls of Thanet) refused to allow development beyond the town itself at the time. Luckily, the narrowness of the ginnels also protected the cottages from straying cows from the cattle market held in the High Street.

Now go down a bit further to where Sheep Street begins, to branch off the High Street. Sheep Street predates the new High Street and was the original main street of the town. The clock above what was once a Manby's Corner shop was installed in 1912 and was one of the very first illuminated clocks in the country, sadly no longer telling the time.

POI2 – The Skipton Walk

As you walk down Sheep Street, you will see what was the town's first Court (fines went straight into the pocket of the Lord of the Manor).

Later, the town Council met here until the current Town Hall was built.

Below the steps was once a single cell for locking up miscreants overnight plus there are the remains of Stocks on both sides of the stairs.

Note the plaque on this building celebrating its history.

On the opposite side of the street to the old town hall is 10, Sheep Street, now W H Smith, within which, over the foyer, is an original, preserved, minstrels' gallery worthy of note.

A little further down Sheep Street go through the archway leading to Victoria Square.

Points of Interest walks in and around West Yorkshire

This area of Victoria Square has all now been modernised, but blends well with old Skipton and note the octagonal shop.

Continue down Victoria Street, keeping to the right of the octagonal shop to the junction at the bottom.

Turn right at the bottom onto Coach Street and across the small bridge over the canal.

Just over the bridge, on the left, descend the steps that take you to an area next to the canal itself.

Turn right along Walbank Wharf.

Be careful, these steps are steep. You can get to this area, avoiding the steps, by continuing a little further on the footpath and entering via the next car park on the left.

POI2 – The Skipton Walk

Here we find a bronze statue of England's most famous fast bowler, Fred Trueman, a true Yorkshireman.

Unveiled in 2010, this sculpture is the work of Graham Ibbeson, who also created the statues or Eric Morecambe, Les Dawson and another cricket legend – Dickie Bird.

Now return to the main road and the bridge, either back up the steps or via the car park.

Either way, note the old fire station building adjacent to the car park.

Once again, cross the bridge, towards the town, and descend the canal side path on the other side taking you to Skipton's Canal Basin.

Keep along the canal side for about 50m and turn left into the square car park, where you will see the White Rose pub and the Pie and Mash shop.

Walk diagonally across the square, as we will turn right here, along Coach Street.

Points of Interest walks in and around West Yorkshire

When you arrive at the end of Coach Street at its T-junction with Belmont Street, turn right across another bridge over the canal (Belmont Bridge).

Cross Belmont Street, and the bridge, and turn left at the first junction to take you along Cavendish Street.

Walk the whole length of Cavendish Street and on the right hand side you will see Skipton Little Theatre. Home of the Skipton Players since 1960, generally believed to be the smallest in the country, the theatre seats a maximum of 72 people.

Turn left along Carleton Street and pass Christ Church on your right.

If it is a dry day and you don't mind walking on the grass, you could take a diversion here to the rear (the other side) of Christ Church where you will find a gravestone for the Calvert family, near the door, where one of the lower entries is for Edwin Calvert, who at the time of his death was the smallest man in England, but if you do indulge please return to your start point on Carleton Street.

25

POI2 – The Skipton Walk

Carry on further along Carleton Street.

You will next cross the canal again, over Gallows Bridge.

Once over the bridge immediately turn right to circumvent the bus station.

When you finish walking around the bus station, you will arrive at Keighley Road. Here, we cross the main road (there is a zebra crossing a few yards to the left) and walk right (away from the town) and after about 40 yards you should meet Sackville Street on the left.

Look up and you will see a balcony on what was once the Liberal Club and nice stone carvings above the Craven Hall.

Walk along Sackville Street, past the Plaza Cinema (was once the Temperance Hall), and past a couple of streets rising steeply to the left, until you meet George Street.

Both of the houses at the bottom of this street have a strange alcove built into them. These are the remnants of the 'laying out board' slits.

When a death occurred in a local family the boards (which were kept locked up in these cupboards) could be laid between two chairs and the body rested in the front room.

Points of Interest walks in and around West Yorkshire

Climb George Street and crossing the road at the top, walk down the equally steep slope of Lambert Street.

At the bottom of Lambert Street, go down The Ginnel and across the bridge at the bottom.

Keep on the tarmac to the left until you once again meet another Ginnel.

Leave the open area and re-enter The Ginnel. Note the Society of Friends (Quaker) meeting house on the right as you pass along the Ginnel.

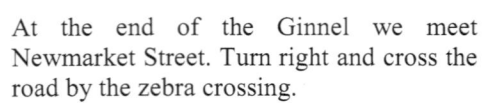

At the end of the Ginnel we meet Newmarket Street. Turn right and cross the road by the zebra crossing.

Keep going along Newmarket Street and soon you will see, on the left, St Andrews Hall (shown here) and Church.

Take the path to the left of the Hall around to the back and through to Otley Street beyond

POI2 – The Skipton Walk

Immediately upon entering Otley Street, through the arch, look to the left and you will see Kipling House.

This was owned by the grandfather of Rudyard Kipling, a Wesleyan Minister in the town, and later by Rudyard's aunts, who ran a private school in the town. Rudyard Kipling was a regular visitor.

Walk past Kipling House towards the town centre and, at the next junction, only a few yards away, you will see the rear entrance to Craven Court - go in.

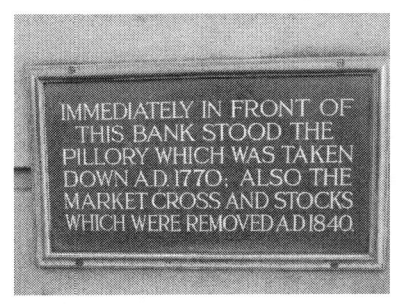

Go through Craven Court covered shopping street and once again back to the High Street.

To the right you will find Barclays Bank a few yards away with this plaque outside.

Turn and proceed down the High Street to the roundabout at the bottom. This area is called Caroline Square, named after Queen Caroline, wife of the Prince Regent, George IV. George had secretly married a Catholic widow, but, under pressure from parliament, bigamously married Princess Caroline of Brunswick. However, he hated her and even banned her from his coronation and attempted to divorce her. It was a public scandal at the time and Skipton renamed this area to show sympathy for Caroline.

Points of Interest walks in and around West Yorkshire

At the bottom of Caroline Square, you will find a plaque on the wall celebrating the birthplace of Thomas Spencer, of Marks and Spencer fame.

Go back along Newmarket Street and then leave Newmarket Street by the first junction on the left, shown here, along Court Lane (it leads once again to the rear of Craven Court).

When you reach the crossroads at the rear of Craven Court, go straight across as shown here and keep going back to the car park where you started.

I hope that you enjoyed the walk.

POI2 – The Skipton Walk

Points of Interest walks in and around West Yorkshire

POI3 – The Ilkley Walk

The walk is an easy stroll around Ilkley town centre.

It is approximately 2 miles but can take up to 1.5 hours because of all the points of interest to view en route.

It is mainly on hard surfaces.

Unfortunately, the walk has some steps and slopes and is not recommended for wheelchairs.

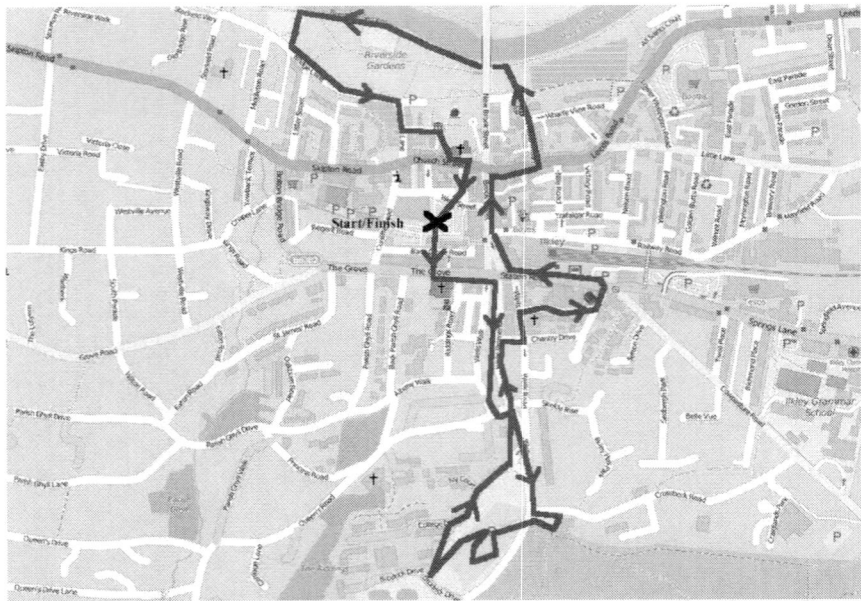

This data is available under the Open Database License and the cartography is licensed as CC BY-SA Visit http://www.openstreetmap.org/copyright for full copyright details © OpenStreetMap contributors

POI3 – The Ilkley Walk

START: The walk starts at the main town centre car park, in the heart of Ilkley. Set your sat nav to LS29 9LB. (This is a Pay and Display car park.)

Leave the car park on the top side.to join Ilkley's main street 'The Grove'.

Cross the road (The Grove) in front of Christchurch and walk left along the side of the church to the next junction.

Turn right at Wells Walk and take the path through the narrow park, alongside the stream.

At the first point where the path divides take the route to the right and underneath a wooden bridge.

32

Points of Interest walks in and around West Yorkshire

Again the path divides and again go right.

Keep on this path until you reach its end and leave the park by the steps to the right.

You are at a junction with Queens Road, which you must cross, and continue your journey uphill along the first road you see directly opposite as shown here.

Keep on this uphill road (do NOT take the small road to the right) and at some point cross the main road to walk up the left hand side.

As you near the next main junction but before you get there, you will see the path shown here, to the left, leading to a large detached building.

Take this path.

The building is called Hillside (was Wells Terrace) and is where Darwin stayed, from 4 Oct 1859 until early December with his family whilst he took the 'water cure' at the nearby Wells House, which we will visit shortly, and where he also stayed for a short time.

POI3 – The Ilkley Walk

Whilst staying in Ilkley, Darwin awaited the publication of his 'On the Origin of Species'. He indulged in the various cures offered in Ilkley, including visiting White Wells, which is above Wells Terrace.

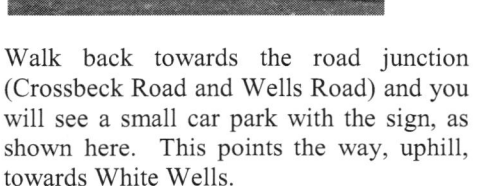

Walk back towards the road junction (Crossbeck Road and Wells Road) and you will see a small car park with the sign, as shown here. This points the way, uphill, towards White Wells.

There has been bathing at White Wells since 1703 when there was a bath to the rear of the premises. This was replaced in 1791 by two baths, one of which is still on display today. Although the water has no significant mineral content, it is the coldness of the water, which stimulates the circulation. White Wells was instrumental in establishing Ilkley as a spa town. A number of large hydros were built in the Ilkley area during the 19th century where people could come to "take the waters", believing all manner of ailments could be cured. Charles Darwin visited Ilkley in 1859 and is believed to have "taken the waters" at White Wells.

Modern day visitors can still use the plunge bath. New Year's Day is the most popular day for this activity, with usually over a hundred plungers throughout the day. However, providing it is quiet enough in the café they can usually open the bath gate should visitors wish to plunge at other times of the year too. Plungers must supply their own bathing costumes and towels and the activity is undertaken at the plunger's own risk! There is no charge for plunging, but bathers can buy a certificate to mark the occasion, throw some loose change into the bath and of course support the café.

White Wells is open on New Year's Day and at weekends 2pm - 5pm during school holidays, particularly the summer holidays. However, White Wells is always open when the flags are flying and closed when the flags are not flying. This walk does not include a diversion to White Wells as the path can be muddy and includes steps and it is a few hundred yards away uphill but, for those fit enough, please break off our walk for a visit and return back to this car park.

Points of Interest walks in and around West Yorkshire

You can just make out White Wells in the distance in this photograph.

Back to the road junction and continue uphill along White Wells Road.

Turn right into Darwin Gardens, the car park, and Millennium Green.

At the entrance to the car park is a monument to Charles Darwin.

Also in the car park you will find the Tree of Life mosaic.

This celebrates Ilkley's Roman heritage and illustrates themes from natural history, again connecting with Darwin.

POI3 – The Ilkley Walk

Back to the Charles Darwin monument and turn right uphill.

You will find yourself at Millennium Green, created to both commemorate the millennium and also the connection with Darwin. A maze is made out of stepping-stones but, when the ground is muddy, still take care, as it is very difficult to leave with clean feet, but great fun for children.

Make your way to the 'notice' at the bottom of Millennium Green and leave the Green by the path shown here, heading uphill.

Take the path to the right, over the wooden bridge.

Alongside this path you will find the Wells House plaque.

Wells House – originally Wells House Hydropathic Establishment – was built in 1856, three years before Darwin made use of its water treatments. It was later converted into a teacher training college and has now been converted into apartments.

Points of Interest walks in and around West Yorkshire

Leave Wells House and take the path to the left, downhill, with the Darwin Gardens on your right.

Continue down this path.

The path joins another one – continue downhill.

The path eventually leads you back to the junction of Queens Road and Wells Road at the top of Wells Walk.

When you return to the main junction of Queens Road and Wells Road, pause to look at the stone steps feature to assist people mounting their horse.

It is placed in the grassy triangular area just above the junction itself, as shown here.

POI3 – The Ilkley Walk

Leave the junction to go down the hill. This time keep to the main road with the gardens to your left.

The road is called Wells Promenade, as shown here.

Halfway down you will find a small side road to the right and here is Chapel House.

Chapel House was built in 1903 as the Wesleyan Assembly Hall.

From 1969 until 1985 it was the Ilkley Methodist Church and has been converted to apartments since 1987.

Go past Chapel House to the junction with Wells Road and turn left downhill.

Further down Wells Road, but before the end, there is another road junction to the right (Whitton Croft Road).

Turn here along this road to the right.

Points of Interest walks in and around West Yorkshire

Immediately on your right you will find the Ilkley Toy Museum.

Continue to the end of Whitton Croft Road and then turn left down the hill until you meet the main road – Station Road.

Turn left.

Here you will find the main Library and the Town Hall (housing the Visitor Information Centre) and Winter Gardens.

The Winter Gardens were completed in 1912, four years after the Town Hall, and has a stage and auditorium, which are still used today.

Some famous speakers here were Adela Pankhurst who addressed a Suffragette meeting here, General Booth spoke to a rally of the Salvation Army and Baden-Powell to a scout rally.

In 1910, cinema equipment was installed but is now no longer in use.

POI3 – The Ilkley Walk

Most Council services have now moved out of Ilkley Town Hall, but the building is still used by Ilkley Parish Council.

It houses Ilkley Visitor Information Centre.

Opposite the Town Hall is the railway station. A major refurbishment of the station took place in November 2011 and it now offers modern facilities to travellers. Cross the road here to walk on the station side towards the town centre (there is a pelican crossing).

Walk along the front of the Railway station towards the large road junction of 'The Grove' and Brook Street.

Turn right at the junction and down the right hand side of Brook Street

At the junction of Brook Street and Church Street turn right along Church Street.

Points of Interest walks in and around West Yorkshire

Cross the main road to enter Weston Road, shown here.

On the left as you walk down Weston Road you will find the old Pinfold. It was the former pound for livestock, built in 1869. It would originally have been gated.

The town Pinder rounded up stray livestock and kept them in the Pinfold until the owner claimed them and paid a fine.

At the bottom of Weston Road is Ilkley Playhouse.

It is owned by Ilkley Players Ltd, a not-for-profit charitable organization.

It is run by an Executive Committee and is staffed almost entirely by volunteers drawn from its membership.

POI3 – The Ilkley Walk

Beyond the end of Weston Road, a path leads straight on towards the river Aire, with steps leading down to the riverside.

Descend these steps and turn left under the roadway, via a tunnel and into Ilkley Park.

To your left, there is a plaque in the park.

It records the fact that the grounds were provided by public subscription in memory of the Ilkley residents who died in the second World War.

Walk along the path, through the gardens, that borders the river.

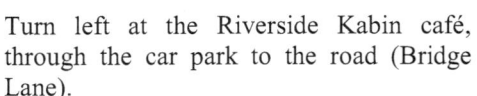

Turn left at the Riverside Kabin café, through the car park to the road (Bridge Lane).

Turn left and walk up Bridge Lane.

Points of Interest walks in and around West Yorkshire

Eventually Bridge Lane turns right through 90 degrees towards the town centre, but still keep on walking on this lane around its bend.

Soon, on the right, you will see a sign pointing to the Manor House.

Follow this sign.

Follow the side street to the left towards the Manor House.

The side street leads to the Manor House, which was until recently a museum and gallery but at the time of writing is now closed to the public.

There is a plaque to explain its importance as a building and its position on the site of an old Roman Fort.

POI3 – The Ilkley Walk

Around the other side of the Manor House is another plaque to show the position of the North Gate of the Roman Fort that lies beneath the grass.

To reach it means walking on the lawn, which might be best avoided if it has been raining.

And down the left side of the Manor House is another plaque giving more details of the fort.

From the front of the Manor House, leave the courtyard via the steps leading to Ilkley All Saints Parish Church, as shown here.

Inside Ilkley All Saints Parish Church stand 3 stone crosses. These Anglo-Saxon crosses, formerly in the churchyard, but now removed into the church to prevent erosion, date to the 8th century.

The shorter bears the figure of a saint on one side, and animals on the other. The most complete one shows St Matthew with the symbolic head of a man, St Mark with the head of a lion, St Luke with the head of an ox and St John with the head of an eagle on the reverse. Christ in Majesty, the third cross, has a stylized vine-scroll pattern and intertwined animals.

Points of Interest walks in and around West Yorkshire

From the church, cross the road via the pelican crossing, to return to the main Ilkley car park.

Go up Hawksworth Street and it will return you to the main car park.

I hope that you enjoyed the walk.

POI3 – The Ilkley Walk

Points of Interest walks in and around West Yorkshire

POI4 – The Hebden Bridge Walk

The walk is an easy stroll around Hebden Bridge town centre.

It is approximately 1.5 miles but can take up to 1 hour because of all the points of interest to view en route.

It is mainly on hard surfaces.

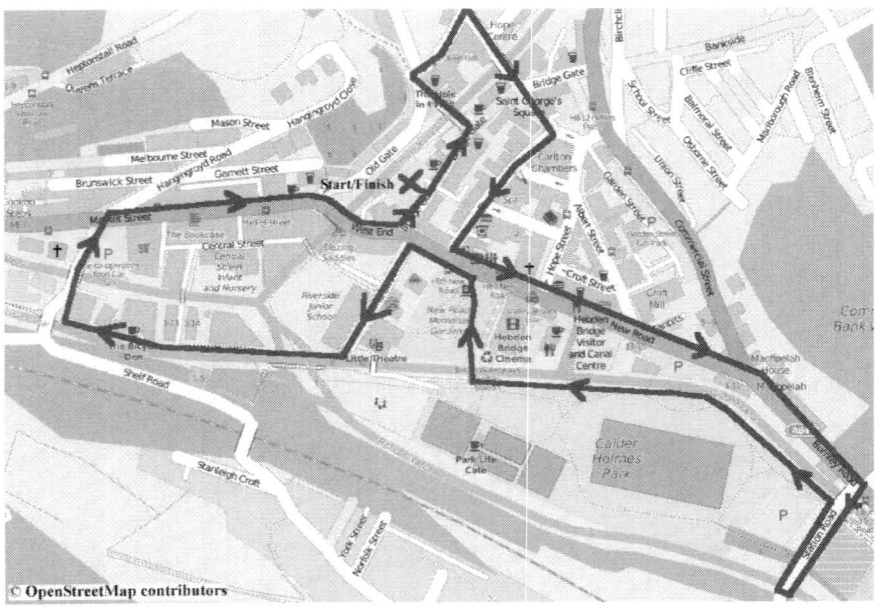

© OpenStreetMap contributors

This data is available under the Open Database license and the cartography is licensed as CC BY-SA
Visit http://www.openstreetmap.org/copyright and opendatacommons.org for full copyright details

POI4 – The Hebden Bridge Walk

START: The walk starts at one of the main town centre car parks, in the heart of Hebden Bridge, in Bridgegate.

Set your sat nav to HX7 8EX. (This is a Pay and Display car park).

Leave the car park and turn left along Bridgegate, towards the Packhorse Bridge and the town centre.

Leave the car park and turn left along Bridgegate, towards the Packhorse Bridge and the town centre. A few yards along Bridgegate, before you arrive at the bridge you will see a plaque on the wall, on the right, which marks the old boundary between the ancient townships of Heptonstall and Wadsworth.

Heptonstall is a village on top of the hill high above Hebden Bridge, but its boundary once extended down to this point and Wadsworth (which is now a civil parish), is also high above Hebden Bridge on an opposing hillside, whose boundary still extends to Hebden Bridge.

The old packhorse route from Halifax to Burnley was mainly on hilltops, but came down to the valley bottom here from Heptonstall to pass over this bridge and then ascend to Wadsworth.

Hebden Bridge was originally just a hamlet based on the wool trade.

When waterpower was needed to industrialise weaving, Hebden Bridge soon had powered mills, as here there is water and steep valley sides in abundance.

Points of Interest walks in and around West Yorkshire

By the 1800s, the industry changed to cotton, especially a kind of strong cotton cloth known as fustian.

Fustian (of which velveteen, corduroy and moleskin are well known examples) is used mainly in menswear. The cloth, woven in strips about 32 inches wide, is changed in appearance by many later processes, the main one of which was having the wefts manually cut (Fustian Cutting) – an extremely laborious process.

Fustian cutting was first adopted here as a trade in the late 18th century, and remained a hand process through the second half of the 19th century. Hebden Bridge became known as 'Trouser Town' (or sometimes Fustianopolis).

From here, a few yards away, you will see the Packhorse Bridge over Hebden Water (which is how Hebden Bridge got its name).

It was built in 1510 and spans Hebden Water. Before that, there were earlier wooden structures dating back as far as 1399.

There are a number of inscriptions on the bridge showing dates of repairs (1602, 1657 and 2011).

Two inscription stones built into the bridge indicate that there were repairs to the bridge in 1602 and 1657.

POI4 – The Hebden Bridge Walk

The first arch was covered by buildings until 1977. It covers what was an outflow of a Bridge Mill waterwheel and was never a span over the river.

There are four alcoves on the bridge that allowed people crossing the bridge to stand back to let the horses pass. The third arch in the bridge is an overflow arch to help prevent flooding.

Over the bridge on your right, you will find the 'Hole in the Wall' public house, dating from 1899, but the site of a number of previous public houses. It is thought that the name derives from cannon-shot damage during the English Civil War.

Opposite you will see a very steep cobbled path leading to Heptonstall. This is called 'The Buttress' and was the old packhorse route.

In 1643, The Buttress and the Packhorse Bridge were the scene of a battle in the English Civil War. The Royalists attempted to capture Heptonstall, at the time a Roundhead stronghold, but failed.

Turn to your right at the base of The Buttress towards the town centre, passing on your left another town centre car park.

It is used on Wednesdays as a regular 'flea' market and on Thursdays as an ordinary market with new goods and food.

There is also a small farmers market on the first and third Sunday of each month, selling homemade bread, cakes, preserves, organic vegetables, crafts and so on.

Points of Interest walks in and around West Yorkshire

We next cross St George's Bridge.

The bridge was built in 1892, in cast iron.

Before crossing the bridge, you will see the Town Hall on your right.

Erected in 1898, it originally included a Fire Station.

The 'Millennium Clock' was installed into Thompson Solicitors' building on Wellington Street, Hebden Bridge in 2000 AD. Funds to pay for the clock were paid by public subscription and presented to the town by the Rotary Club of Hebden Bridge. The dial is the Rotary Club symbol of a cogwheel, with the planets rotating around it, whilst the sun is shown symbolically both above and below the dial.

Once across the bridge you enter St George's Square.

In St George's Square, there is the Fustian Sundial. The gnomon represents a fustian cutter's needle, and the design cast in bronze at its base shows a fustian cutter at work. The sculptor is Mike Newell.

Also there are carved stone bollards located near the sundial. They are the work of local sculptor Mike Williams.

POI4 – The Hebden Bridge Walk

Looking back, Bridge Mill can be seen in the square. This is the site of a mill, which predates the town itself.

It was originally a water-powered manorial corn mill dating from 1314, whose diverted water returned to the river under the first arch of the Packhorse Bridge we viewed earlier.

The mill was occupied by Royalist troops in 1643 during the English Civil War. It now houses shops and a cafe and, inside, there is a restored waterwheel. The current building dates back mainly to the late 18th Century although some remnants of the original building still exist inside.

The mill chimney dates to 1820 when steam power took over from water

The White Lion hotel stands next to Bridge Mill.

Built in 1657 this is one of the oldest buildings in the town, originally King's Farm – note the date stone over the front door. Also, the inn was used as a popular stop on the Halifax to Rochdale stagecoach run.

A horse mill for grinding malt stood opposite the inn from around 1618.

Go through the tunnel, shown here, past shops and into a car park.

This car park was once the site of another inn 'The White Horse', and the owner, a William Patchett, built a road alongside (which is now the road through the square today) which diverted trade away from his brother's hotel 'The White Lion' which we have just looked at.

Points of Interest walks in and around West Yorkshire

From here, we see Hollins Toll Bar House. This was built as a tollhouse for the first Turnpike Road into Hebden Bridge in 1786 but was only in use for 20 years.

The walled up windows in the end of the house were once used to watch for approaching wagons and coaches.

The large vertical stone at the corner of the building was probably the support for the tollgate itself.

To your right is the old Hebden Bridge Co-operative building.

The Co-operative movement was formalised in Rochdale in 1844 and four years later, the Hebden Bridge Co-op was formed.

The existing building dates from 1876 with expansion in 1889 – both dates can be seen on the building.

The Co-op was a huge retailer and employer in town, having 128 employees in 1948.

However, the society went bankrupt in 1967 after an employee embezzled funds.

Opposite the old Co-op building is a baker's shop, which has an unusual top storey, which was a water tank originally designed to serve the Co-op building.

Make your way down Crown Street to the main Burnley Road and turn left at the end.

POI4 – The Hebden Bridge Walk

The Picture House.

Built in 1921 and restored in 1978, The Picture House seats 493 people.

As well as films, it hosts concerts and other live events.

Hope Baptist Church.

Built in 1857 for the Particular Baptists.

A curious plaque is mounted on Hope Baptist Church.

Curious because John Fawcett passed away some 40 years before this church was built.

The Marina is found on the opposite side of the main road.

It was originally built in 1893, as a canal-loading bay.

The Rochdale Canal itself was opened in 1798. The Marina was once filled in to become a garage but was restored 1985-87.

The Tourist Information Office can be found nearby.

Points of Interest walks in and around West Yorkshire

The town is particularly prone to flooding.

This plaque, on a wall of the Marina area, relates to June 2000, but further floods have occurred in 2009, twice in 2012 and on Boxing day, 2015.

This marker, near to the plaque above, was erected at Hebden Bridge marina to commemorate the start of the twin town partnership with Stadt Warstein, Germany, in 1995.

It roughly translates to ...
'TO COMMEMORATE THE START OF THE TWIN TOWN ARRANGEMENT - HEBDEN ROYD GB -WARSTEIN – D 5 - 11 – 1995'.

Keep walking, past the marina, away from the town.

The Brick House.

Built from hand-made bricks of various sizes and dating to the early 19th Century.

The Brick House is a curiosity, as most property was stone built in this area.

Keep walking away from the town.

PO14 – The Hebden Bridge Walk

This area is named Machpelah after Abraham's burial place in the Bible, by the Rev John Fawcett, when he bought the land to build the houses.

He was Minister of Wainsgate Chapel in 1764.

He was offered a position in London, but after packing to leave was so moved by local people's affection that he changed his mind and stayed here as minister of the Ebenezer Chapel, which we will see later.

The first 3 houses were built about 1804 for Rev Fawcett and his family to live in when he retired in 1805 (it is thought that he lived in No 12).

He wanted to be buried in a family vault on the hillside behind (hence the name of the area) but an increased demand for buildings meant that he was buried at Wainsgate Chapel.

It is thought that the first house was later altered by the addition of many windows to make the top two floors into Fustian Cutters' workshops. Here they sheared cloth with special knives to give it a corduroy feel – hence the need for lots of windows giving as much light as possible.

Machpelah House was built by Steven Fawcett, his grandson (1842 – date on chimney).

You can see a blocked-in archway, originally for horse and coach access.

Points of Interest walks in and around West Yorkshire

On the opposite side of the road from Machpelah House, and further away from the town, you turn right across Princess Bridge over the Rochdale canal.

After crossing the bridge, pause on the towpath to the left and look back.

You will see that the bridge has been widened on one side (late 19th Century) by the addition of a steel girder but you can still see the stone arch of the original beneath it.

Notice the wooden roller to prevent towropes, wearing and breaking on the stones.

The next bridge is Victoria Bridge (late 19th Century replacing a previous wooden one) spanning the river Calder.

Look for the mason's marks on the left hand turret.

Over the bridge and to your left is the town's railway station.

Hebden Bridge Station was built by Lancashire & Yorkshire Railway in 1893 including engineering by George Stephenson.

In 1841, the Lancashire and Yorkshire Railway opened its line through the Calder Valley, further improving transport links. The Station is Grade II listed and it was renovated in 1997.

POI4 – The Hebden Bridge Walk

Back to the canal and turn left into Calder Holmes Park. As you enter, the first row of trees marks the Coronation of George VI in 1937 and those, that border the playing field, commemorate the Silver Jubilee of Elizabeth II.

On your journey round the park, you will find a plaque, on stone, to also commemorate her Silver Jubilee.

Take the path to the right at this point, through the park alongside the canal.

There is a cafe and play areas to explore within the park.

Exit the park by way of the first bridge you encounter that crosses the canal.

You can climb the steps that greet you or walk further and return to the bridge via this slope.

You are now within the Memorial Gardens and here there is a plaque to commemorate HMS Bradford, the ship adopted by Hebden Bridge in 1942 during Warship Week.

The plaque also shows the Packhorse Bridge and the ruined medieval church at Heptonstall.

Points of Interest walks in and around West Yorkshire

Leave the park, passing the War Memorial, and turn left along Burnley Road.

Exiting the park, we find Holme House built in 1826. It was originally a private residence but later became a doctor's surgery. Turn left here.

The nearby Post Office was opened in 1930 and has an arched doorway in Tudor style, pinnacled gables and mullioned windows.

Next to the Post Office, you find The Trades Club, now a music venue and bar.

Built in 1924, it was originally home to the Trades Council, which looked after the interests of weavers, dyers etc in the cloth trades.

Opposite to the Trades Club is Riverside School, erected 1909 as a secondary school and entitled 'The Grammar School' by Head Teacher Herbert Howarth in 1926. It became a Junior School in 1965.

POI4 – The Hebden Bridge Walk

The nearby Little Theatre was formed in 1924 and moved to its current purpose-built premises in 1993.

Passing the Little Theatre on your left walk up the slope to the canal side and turn right along the canal.

Before setting off down the canal, you might like to first cross the canal and walk a short distance down the other side until the path stops after about 100 yards to take the view from the left side of the aqueduct that takes the canal over the river.

If you do take in that view then you must return to this spot to progress further down the canal.

This is Black Pit Aqueduct, which has four 25ft arches carrying the canal over the river Calder. There is a date stone on the centre pier with a sculpted head.

Just before the first bridge you reach, is this building, which was once The Neptune Inn.

Now turn right before the bridge, which is the Neptune Bridge.

Points of Interest walks in and around West Yorkshire

Cross to the nearby road and towards the town centre (you should see the Cooperative Supermarket to your right).

Ahead is Barker's Terrace (note the three storeys, with the elaborately carved lintels).

Walking back into town, we come across the former Ebenezer Chapel, built in 1777. It is fronted by a beautiful sundial. It was the main chapel of the Particular Baptists until Hope Chapel was built. It is currently an Arts Centre. Built in 1777 by John Fawcett for the grand sum of 450 pounds, Ebenezer Chapel at the town end of the street now houses Heart Gallery.

Further into town, we cross West End Bridge, built in 1771 to carry the new turnpike road from Halifax to Todmorden and bypassing the Packhorse Bridge we saw earlier.

(The town was given a county grant of £270 to rebuild the Packhorse Bridge but spent the money on this bridge instead).

Turn left into Bridgegate and we are back at the car park, where the walk began.

I hope that you enjoyed the walk.

POI4 – The Hebden Bridge Walk

Points of Interest walks in and around West Yorkshire

POI5 – The Haworth Walk

The walk is an easy stroll around Haworth town centre.

It is approximately 1.5 miles but can take up to 1 hour because of all the points of interest to view en route.

It is mainly on hard surfaces but there are steps and slopes and is not wheelchair friendly.

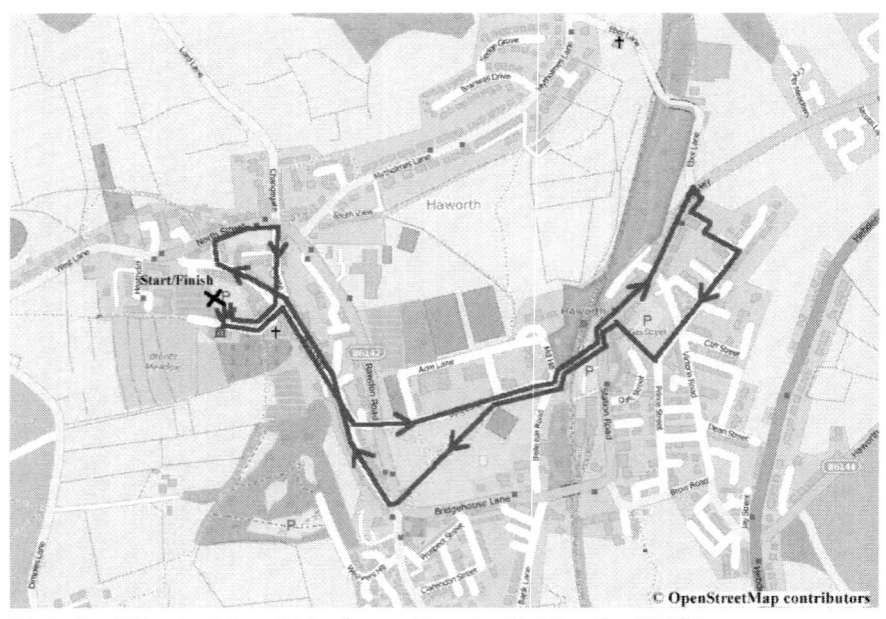

© OpenStreetMap contributors

This data is available under the Open Database license and the cartography is licensed as CC BY-SA
Visit http://www.openstreetmap.org/copyright and opendatacommons.org for full copyright details

PO15 – The Haworth Walk

START: The walk starts at one of the main town centre car parks, at the top of the town, nearest to the Brontë Parsonage.

Set your sat nav to BD22 8DS. (This is a Pay and Display car park.)

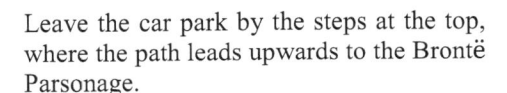

Leave the car park by the steps at the top, where the path leads upwards to the Brontë Parsonage.

You probably want to visit the Parsonage, as most people do.

You could start or end your walk with the visit, but either way you should first buy your ticket from the ticket office to the right of the parsonage, as shown here.

The parsonage closes in January, other than on New Year's Day.

Whether you visit the parsonage itself or not, we now enter the front garden, which is free to enter.

The extension to the right was added after the Brontës had left.

Points of Interest walks in and around West Yorkshire

Within the garden, opposite to the parsonage itself, is a stone showing the location of the original gate to the graveyard. The Brontës were buried within the church building and not in the graveyard itself.

Leaving the parsonage, go downhill towards the church and town centre.

This building on your left is a school, which Patrick Brontë was instrumental in having built in 1832.

There are a number of plaques (old and new) that celebrate its history . . .

High above the door is this old plaque:

'This National Church Sunday School is under the management of Trustees, of whom the Incumbent for the time being is one: and was erected AD1832 by Voluntary Subscription and by a Grant from the National Society in London.
"Train up a child, in the way he should go, and when he is old he will not depart from it" Prov XXII. 6'

A second plaque adds that all the Brontë children taught at the school and also that it was the location of Charlotte's wedding reception in 1854.

POI5 – The Haworth Walk

Finally, a third plaque tells of the restoration of the school in 1966.

Walk further down the path towards the church. Before you reach the church, there is an entry on the right to the graveyard and you will find this plaque.

It shows the locations of graves associated with the Brontës but none of the actual family members, most of these being buried within the church itself.

The other graves identified are of (a) John Brown 1804-1855, the Haworth sexton, who was a close friend of Branwell Brontë and (b) Tabitha "Tabby" Aykroyd, who was for 30 years servant to the Brontës until her death in 1855 at the age of 84.

There is an old font from the church, used by P Brontë, now in a garden below the graveyard on the far side of the church close to the path, with 'W Grimshaw' inscribed on it. William Grimshaw (1708-1763) worked closely with the Wesley brothers who founded the Methodist church movement.

He was Rector of the church in Haworth from 1742 until his death in 1763.

He was an evangelist and was even known to leave the church whilst psalms were sung to search the churchyard, street and even the alehouses to round up the sinners.

In one long sermon, he said "I may talk to you till my tongue is as small as a sparble. You will all go to hell after all" (a sparble was a small nail used in clog making).

Points of Interest walks in and around West Yorkshire

This is the grave of Timothy Feather 1825-1910 (known as Owd Timmy locally) last of the hand weavers, making Twill cotton.

The grave is at the bottom of the graveyard on the left, looking uphill.

In the 18th century, all weaving was done at home (upstairs) by hand weavers, but the introduction of mechanisation and powered mills led to its decline by the mid 19th century. Timothy Feather continued well past the date that all others had stopped.

St. Michael and All Angels Church.

The church is usually open and you should take the opportunity to explore the inside, where Patrick Brontë was the curate, and where is located the Brontë family vault, and the 'American window'. (This stained glass window is an American Memorial to Charlotte Brontë donated by Thomas Hockley.)

After visiting the church go further down towards the town centre, keeping close to the church as shown here.

POI5 – The Haworth Walk

Leaving the church behind and down a few steps you should find yourself in this busy open area at the top of the Main Street.

Looking back towards the church you will see this shop, opposite the current Post Office.

This shop was the original Post Office from where the Brontës sent their original manuscripts.

Next to this shop, you will see the old Stocks. Stocks like this were very common in English villages.

They were used to punish wrongdoers who were trapped by their ankles so that they could be pelted with rotten vegetables, etc by the locals.

To your right is the Black Bull public house.

This was a regular haunt of Branwell Brontë, where he had his own corner chair (now in the Parsonage museum).

Points of Interest walks in and around West Yorkshire

Outside the Black Bull, you will find this plaque celebrating Branwell as a 19th century regular.

BUT – spot the mistake.

Opposite is the current Apothecary shop, previously the local Co-op and in the days of the Brontës a druggist shop from where Branwell bought his supplies of laudanum. Laudanum contained 10% opium.

An archway that used to be called Gauger's Croft is to the right of the Apothecary.

A Gauger was an exciseman whose job was to stop illegal alcohol smuggling or brewing.

The archway is linked to a row of terraces, which were once called Brandy Row, so around here maybe they stored such spirits.

We now set off down the Main Street.

The cobbles are known as 'setts'.

POI5 – The Haworth Walk

Also – you will find examples of 'Coal Holes' (pronounced 'Coiloiles') where, as the name tells you, cottages stored the coal for their fires.

Look out for ginnels such as the one shown here.

A ginnel is a passageway between terraced houses (often covered) and examples can be found on the Main Street of Haworth.

Half way down the Main Street look out for a signpost pointing to the Railway Station and turn left off the main street at this point.

Go down past the cobbled beginning towards the Railway Station.

Just after the cobbles end, look to your right and you will see that the retaining wall has been built incorporating what was once part of a cottage. This is not unique as another example exists near Halifax.
(see another of the walks POI1 Wainhouse).

Points of Interest walks in and around West Yorkshire

You soon come to a main road.

Cross via the zebra crossing just to your left and continue downhill into Butt Lane as shown here.

On your left you will see what was once Haworth primary school opened in 1897, closed in 2001 and is now residential accommodation.

After the old school is the former Mechanics Institute.

This was founded in 1849, not as a Social Club with bar, etc as you see now – but as a place of learning, including its own library for lectures and other intellectual pursuits and probably attended by Patrick Brontë, as previously he had been a member of the Keighley Mechanics Institute.

He may have been instrumental in its creation as he was very keen on the local population improving itself.

Note the 'weavers cottage' at the bottom of Butt Lane on your left.

The row of windows on the top floor is typical of weavers' houses.

The weaving took place on this floor with the windows built to allow in as much light as possible.

PO I5 – The Haworth Walk

Continue down to the end of Butt Lane and turn left where you will see ahead a bridge across the railway line.

Cross this bridge to Haworth Station.

If you are lucky you may see one of the steam trains which use this line. This is the Worth Valley Railway.

Once over the bridge, the station is to your left and please take a look around. It is free to enter and you are encouraged to take a trip on the trains, either now or at the end of your walk.

Carry on along the main road past the Railway Station for some 800 meters, on the left hand side, until you come to Ebor Lane, where you will find this stone plaque.

It reads

" CAUTION AND PUBLIC NOTICE This is a Private Occupation Road between Oakworth Hall and Ebor Lane Top and is the Private Freehold of JOHN CRAVEN, of BERRIDGE HOUSE IN BINGLEY. NO PERSON CAN lawfully pass hereon without his leave. Except persons going on Ordinary Business to and from the Estates of the late HIRAM CRAVEN of DOCKROYD, DECEASED, and of the said JOHN CRAVEN And persons going on like purposes between Oakworth Hall and LOWER LAITH, the LODGE, and the Oakworth Corn Mill Farm, the property of JOHN WRIGHT of LOWER LAITH and between OAKWORTH and the LOWER PROVIDENCE MILL the property of CALEB LEACH of HALIFAX. All other Persons passing hereon after this NOTICE will be treated as Willfull Trespassers.
Berridge House, Bingley   July 1843 JOHN CRAVEN"

Points of Interest walks in and around West Yorkshire

This lane was for private use only and another identical plaque exists over the doorway of a house at the top of the lane to stop unwanted visitors going down the lane too. Our walk does not encourage such a visit as the lane is quite dangerous to pass as it lacks any pavements, but if you feel the urge then by all means have a look at the other plaque and return here, but take care whilst travelling the lane.

We now turn around and head back towards the town centre.

Across the main road you will see the now derelict Mill Hey Primitive Methodist Chapel. It was opened in 1870 but closed in 1954.

Before crossing the main road glance up at the doorway of the first building on your right. This is Haworth Masonic Hall (Lodge of the Three Graces) built in 1907 and still in use today.

The lodge has moved a couple of times since Branwell Brontë was Secretary when it was in Lodge Street, just off Main Street.

Cross the road and take the path up the side of the Chapel.

73

POI5 – The Haworth Walk

Upon leaving the path you then climb the road shown here up to Prince Street.

Walk along Prince Street.

Prince Street, along with the surrounding streets, was originally built in 1890 to house workers for the mills – a new town away from Main Street. Now they are all modernised, but note the steepness of the side streets.

Soon Prince Street intersects with Aspley Street. Look to your left up the hill and there is the new Brontë Cinema (currently a garage).

This was open from 1921-1956.

The walk now takes you down Aspley Street, as shown, towards the town centre.

You will meet the main road again opposite to the Conservative Club.

Water was seen pouring out of the downstairs windows during the flood of 2004 (and previously in 1946).

74

Points of Interest walks in and around West Yorkshire

To your left you will once again see the Railway Station.

Cross the road via the Zebra crossing.

Haworth and Haworth railway station have been used as settings for numerous period films and TV series.

They include The Railway Children (starring Jenny Agutter), Yanks (starring Richard Gere and Vanessa Redgrave), and Alan Parker's film version of Pink Floyd's The Wall (starring Bob Geldof) plus "Wild Child" (starring Emma Roberts).

Please explore the station if you did not do so earlier – there is no charge to look around.

Then retrace your earlier steps up the path and over the bridge to the left of the station.

Now comes the difficult climb back up Butt Lane – but this this time we only walk less than half way up it as we soon divert through the park.

Look for this gate to your left.

It is here that we leave Butt Lane and enter Haworth Central Park.

POI5 – The Haworth Walk

Beyond the Bandstand take the path to the left.

La Famille De Cuivre
(The Copper Family) 2014 by Craig Dyson, born Haworth 1990.

Made of 28000 donated 2ps to create a legacy of the Yorkshire Grand Depart 2014 (Tour de France).

As we leave the park, we see Haworth Old Hall.

Dating back to 1580, this is one of the oldest buildings in Haworth. In the 17th century the Emmott family owned the hall (plus most of Haworth).

There are two mile-long tunnels leading from the cellars, thought to have been used as escape routes (from the religious persecutions of the Roman Catholics). One runs to the Parish Church.

Now we will climb Main Street, back towards the car park and the end of the walk.

The 2014 Tour de France cycle race route included going up Main Street, on these cobbles!!

Points of Interest walks in and around West Yorkshire

Note this doorway (not one for people to enter) which has above it the arm for a winch to raise and lower goods into and out of the building.

We return to the top of Main Street. You will see the Old White Lion public house dead ahead.

Room 7 is supposed to be haunted by the ghost of Lily Cove, where she died on 11th June 1906.

Lily, aged 21, from East London travelled the country with Captain Frederick Bidmead, a stunt balloonist, performing at galas where she jumped from a balloon and parachuted to the ground.

The attempt was supposed to take place during the local gala on Saturday 9th June 1906 but, because of problems with the balloon, it was postponed until the evening of Monday 11th and took place on West Lane football field. This time there were no problems and the balloon ascended to about 700ft and Lily jumped and her parachute opened normally.

She descended to about 100ft and then was observed to wriggle from the parachute harness and plummet to the ground where she was severely injured and was taken back to her room at the Old White Horse, where she was pronounced dead.

PO15 – The Haworth Walk

At the inquest, a verdict of 'death by misadventure' was reached, but it was speculated that Lily, realising that she was drifting towards the nearby Ponden reservoir and as she couldn't swim, she deliberately freed herself from the parachute misjudging her current height from the ground.

Her grave is at Haworth Cemetery, Cemetery Road next to Penistone Hill Country Park and the headstone shows the balloon and parachute attached.

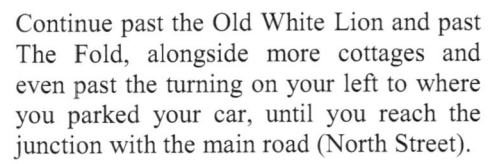

Continue past the Old White Lion and past The Fold, alongside more cottages and even past the turning on your left to where you parked your car, until you reach the junction with the main road (North Street).

Across the road, you will see West Lane Baptist Church. Haworth's first Baptist chapel, this is an important building in the Baptist revival in West Yorkshire.

Earlier we saw an old font with the name W Grimshaw on it. Grimshaw was a friend of John Wesley who formed the Methodist church movement and wanted Grimshaw as is successor.

But it was one of Grimshaw's converts, James Hartley, who broke away from the Anglican Church, who had the original Church built here, with this latest replacement being built in 1844. Hartley and his wife Anne are buried here, their gravestones are immediately in front of the building.

Points of Interest walks in and around West Yorkshire

Do not cross the road, but turn right here and walk down North Street.

Along the way, you will see yet another 'Ginnel' and on the pavement is this 'flag' (flat paving stone).

The writing became smaller and smaller until the sculptor finally gave up – so we will now never know who laid the flags.

Pass a car park on your right and then turn right back towards Main Street.

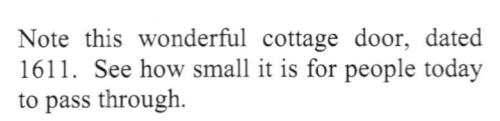

Note this wonderful cottage door, dated 1611. See how small it is for people today to pass through.

Finally, you arrive back at the car park. I hope that you enjoyed the walk.

Points of Interest walks in and around West Yorkshire

POI6 – The Saltaire Walk

The walk is an easy stroll around the area of Saltaire, West Yorkshire.

It is approximately 1.5 miles but can take up to 1 hour because of all the points of interest to view en route.

It is on hard surfaces and, although there are some steps, these can be avoided and so is wheelchair friendly although there are cobbles and some slopes.

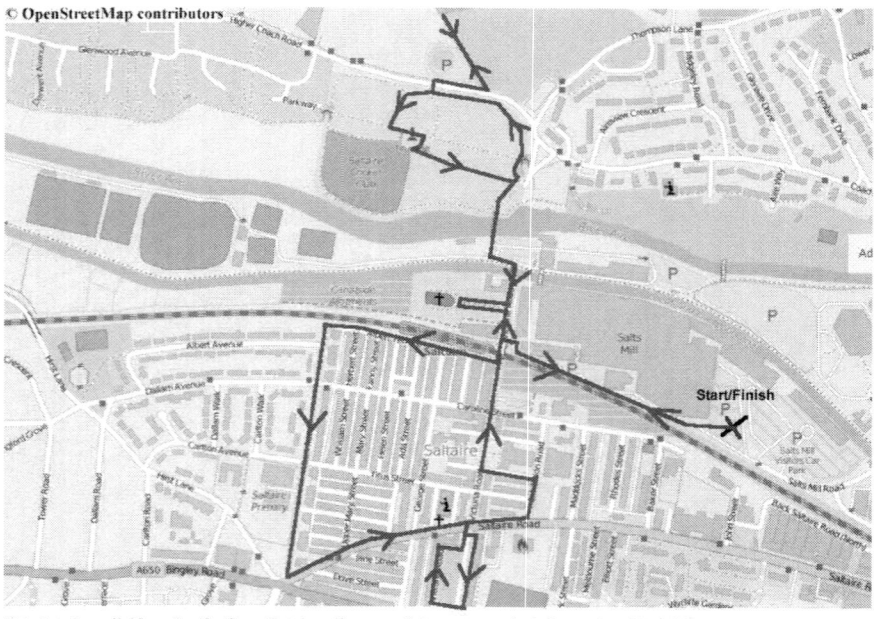

This data is available under the Open Database license and the cartography is licensed as CC BY-SA
Visit http://www.openstreetmap.org/copyright and opendatacommons.org for full copyright details

POI6 – The Saltaire Walk

Titus Salt (1803-1876) came to Bradford in 1822, when his father moved there, and started a wool merchant business, where he worked from 1825. In 1829, he began his own worsted stuff manufacturing business.

By 1850, he was probably the richest man in Bradford and it is then that he formed the idea of building Saltaire (built between 1851-1871). This was to be a huge mill with accommodation, and facilities for recreation, hospital and schools for all the workers.

Saltaire is laid out in a grid pattern and with no public houses, pawnshop nor police. It was heralded as a great success and Titus was made a Baronet in 1869 and Emperor Napoleon III even made him a member of the Legion of Honour.

Set your Sat Nav to BD17 7EF but when it tells you that you have reached your destination, keep going along Salts Mill Road following the brown signs - you'll pass a big red brick chimney on your left as you cross the canal and The Waterfront, an office building, on your right, then you'll see the mill at the end of the road.

You can also visit by train as there is a station on the opposite side of the road to the mill.

START: The walk starts at Salts Mill, where there is a very large free car park as shown here (but it is only open between 10.00am and 5.30pm weekdays and 10.00am and 6.00pm weekends). This is the first car park you meet on the right before passing any buildings, but if it is a weekend keep going right to the mill itself as the normally-reserved parking there is free to use.

If you have a disabled badge then also keep going right to the mill itself, any day of the week, as there are a number of disabled bays just outside the mill door.

This is a circular walk and upon our return to the mill you are encouraged to go in and look at the Hockney exhibition, the shops and other facilities within (it is free to enter). Please be patient and wait until your return.

Points of Interest walks in and around West Yorkshire

Walk past the side entrance to the mill. Note the two very tall towers which flank the tunnel entrance; they were intentionally designed to mimic those of Osborne House, the residence of Prince Albert and Queen Victoria, on the Isle of Wight (Salt was an admirer of Prince Albert).

The mill, opened in 1853, made cloth from alpaca wool and mohair from the Angora goat. Titus came across some alpaca wool in 1836 in a Liverpool warehouse, which he bought and perfected into cloth in an earlier mill in Bradford. It was upon this that the mill and village of Saltaire were founded.

Walk to the corner of the mill and turn to the right and pass through a large gate as shown here.

You will see a tunnel entrance here, opposite to the entrance to the mill yard.

This tunnel leads underneath Victoria Road to the mill's Dining Hall. It was by this route that the workers from the mill visited their canteen.

Either ascend the steps to the left of the tunnel (keep right) or, if using a wheelchair, go to the right towards the main mill entrance.

You arrive at the road that slopes from left to right (Victoria Road). On the opposite side of the road, you will see the building shown here.

PO16 – The Saltaire Walk

This is the main mill Dining Hall (for the workers), who would have entered via the tunnel rather than by crossing the road. This accommodated up to 800 people and about 600 workers took breakfast and about 700 took dinner daily.

Within the circle above the door is the Salt crest (the bird is an ostrich with a horseshoe in its beak – the ostrich represents willing obedience and serenity and the horseshoe is for good luck and protection). At the time of building, Salt was not entitled to a coat of arms – he just invented one for himself. Salt did not run the Dining Hall, but charged his workers 5% per annum (£180) on the £3600 it cost him to build it.

Cross Victoria Road and, looking back at the mill, you will see the main entrance.

Opposite to the mill entrance, you will see the Congregational Church (now the United Reformed Church), which we will visit now.

Before the church was built, the congregation met at 10 Caroline Street (1854) and then in the Dining Hall (1856). Opened on 13th April 1859, it was the first public building erected in Saltaire and seats 600. It is richly decorated with coloured marble in the Italian style. Heavy draperies had to be introduced into the church to solve a problem with the acoustics. To the left as you approach it, on the outside, is the Mausoleum, where Titus himself is buried along with some members of his family.

The Salt family occupied the 3rd pew from the front on the left. There is also a balcony built at the insistence of Salt's wife, Caroline, for the family, but Salt preferred to sit amongst his workers. The story goes that Salt bought two massive chandeliers and had them hung so that they obscured the view from that balcony, as a joke on his wife. Note the initials TS above every window (you will see this again and again on most buildings).

Points of Interest walks in and around West Yorkshire

Return to Victoria Road. Just below the entrance from Victoria Road to the church is a building for the Stable Block and Office House.

The Office House was occupied by a butler, cook-housekeeper and a general servant to cater for the Salt family, when in the village. The stables were for horses for the domestic use of the family only – not connected with work in the mill.

Across Victoria Road, you see New Mill (1868) – a spinning mill created to make use of the spare steam power.

The chimney is a copy of the campanile of the Venetian church of Santa Maria Gloriosa. It was designed so as to not spoil the view from Victoria Road. Unfortunately, its Bell Tower had to be replaced in 1937 by the current cowl as it became unsafe.

Go down to the bottom of Victoria Road, keeping to the left, and you will arrive at the bridge, as shown here.

Upstream of the bridge, to your left, there is a waterside pub and, across the river, you will see Roberts Park and a distant cricket ground. To the right is a manmade weir to provide water to the mill, where you can often find a heron fishing. Now cross the bridge.

PO16 – The Saltaire Walk

The Lodge, listed Grade II, stands at the main entrance to the Park. Its Gothic Revival architectural style is used throughout Saltaire Village. It is likely that the park keeper would have lived in the Lodge - the bell on the southern gable would be rung at sunset to inform Park visitors that it was time to leave. In the 1920s, it was home to the Head Gardener.

Roberts Park opened, with a great ceremony, one evening in 1871 as 'Saltaire Park'. All the employees attended (the mill was closed early) and there were speeches and bands.

The park was for the use of the villagers, but with many rules – No music, singing, preaching, lecture or public discussion etc, no stone throwing, disorderly conduct, bad language, gambling, begging, alcohol, smoking (in the alcoves) or spitting – and the playgrounds not to be used on Sundays. This is the plaque on the gatehouse.

Sir James Roberts changed the name to Roberts Park when he became owner of Saltaire in 1893. In January 1920 he gave the park to Bradford as a memorial to his late son Bertram.

This the East Shelter. Walk past this shelter and keep to the path, which goes around the park.

There are three shelters, all listed Grade II, originally containing wooden bench seats, around the walls, and the West Shelter even had men's public toilets beneath it.

Points of Interest walks in and around West Yorkshire

You will come across the North Shelter, after which we leave the park.

Cross the main road by the Zebra Crossing

Head across the car park – there is a gate on the other side of the central island.

Turn left after going through the gate and you will see the Shipley Glen Tramway – which we will now visit. This cable tramway was opened to the public on 18th May 1895. It was originally powered by gas but was converted to electricity in 1928. The track has a gauge of 20" and there are two tracks with a tramcar on each line.

It is open at weekends 12.00-16.00 (Sundays only in winter) – take the opportunity to enjoy this pleasure from another age.

Retrace your steps to the park and follow the path down but to the right as shown here.

PO16 – The Saltaire Walk

Keep going down the path towards the bandstand and statue.

At the bottom of the path, on the right, you will find this plinth, which reads ...

"Presented by the Shipley & District Friendly & Trade Societies in Commemoration of their First Fete & Gala in aid of the local Charities held on this park July 4th 1885".

To the left is the bandstand.

The original bandstand was demolished during the second world war.

The park was restored in 2010 with a new bandstand and refurbished promenade terraces, alcove seats and planting.

Also, here you find the statue of Titus.

Commissioned by J Roberts, who had taken over the firm in 1893.

Points of Interest walks in and around West Yorkshire

Around the base of the statue, you will find plaques of the Alpaca and Angora Goat (from which comes mohair).

The initial success of the mill came from these.

Go down the steps from the statue of Titus and in front of the park cafe, you will find this statue to again celebrate the alpacas.

The Half Moon Pavilion is the centrepiece of the Park and is listed Grade II. It was originally a Tea Room, with a balcony area on its roof, on which stands F Derwent Wood's 1903 statue of Sir Titus Salt. The Pavilion is now used by Saltaire Cricket Club for storage and as a café.

We will now leave the park and once again cross the bridge over the river, following the path shown here and return up Victoria Road, past the church and passing over the railway bridge and turning right into the next street - Albert Terrace.

PO16 – The Saltaire Walk

Albert Terrace.

This street, being still cobbled, looks much as it did in the 1870s. Named after Prince Albert (plus Albert Road into which we turn next) – a man much admired by Titus.

The main street in Saltaire is named after Queen Victoria, and the architects Lockwood and Mawson both have streets named after them.

Titus started to use his children's names for streets, in order of birth (he had 11 children).

One street was named Caroline (his wife), also Dove, Jane and Katherine (daughters-in-law) with Shirley, Constance, Gordon and Harold (grandchildren) and finally Fern, Daisy and Myrtle (his wife's maids).

As we pass Amelia Street, it is worth mentioning that at the top of this street originally were the Public Baths and Wash Houses, now demolished.

Titus refused to allow people to hang their washing outside and so provided an alternative in the Wash Houses, with rubbing and boiling tubs, centrifugal spinners, hot air blowers and a drying closet.

Use of the Wash Houses or baths was not free, which was greatly disliked, especially on dry sunny days when, without the rule, the workers would have been able to dry their clothes for nothing.

When Titus moved out of Saltaire, the rule went too and the buildings fell into disuse and were converted to housing in 1894. However, people refused to live there and they too were demolished.

Points of Interest walks in and around West Yorkshire

Keep walking down Albert Terrace past Fanny Street.

At the end of Albert Terrace turn left into Albert Road.

We now enter part of the residential area, which in 1871 had 775 houses, 45 Almshouses, and a population of 4,389.

The houses were designed for different grades of his workforce – note the difference in size of houses as you leave Albert Terrace and progress up Albert Road (called Overlookers houses).

Salt's senior staff were reluctant to live in Saltaire (as was Salt himself) despite the superior accommodation and, in 1871, some of the houses in Albert Road were rented to people not connected to the mill. None of the houses were 'back-to-back' which was a common style elsewhere. Today all the houses are privately owned.

Walking up Albert Road, we see on the right Albert Road Board Schools – Infants – opened 1878, with 16 classrooms with both boys and girls in each class taught by an adult female teacher.

On the day it opened, there were 314 half timers present, 9 Assistants plus Head Mistress, Sewing mistress and a drill sergeant.

Today it has over 400 pupils (all full time).

PO16 – The Saltaire Walk

At the top of Albert Road, we meet the main road (A657 to Shipley).

Saltaire itself continues on the other side of the main road too, as you can see here, with Jane Street.

Our walk turns left along the main road at this point.

Saltaire Methodist Church is on your left. Yes, this is a fairly new building, but on the same site as the original chapel that Salt built, demolished in 1970.

When we meet the junction with Victoria Road, you need to cross the main A657 by the nearby zebra crossing and walk uphill on Victoria Road.

The first building on the left in Victoria Road was originally the hospital. Now it is 3 storeys but started as a 2 storey building – opened as it says both above and on the door, in 1868.

It originally had 9 beds and was manned by a 'competent surgeon' and a live-in nurse.

Points of Interest walks in and around West Yorkshire

Enlarged to 17 beds in 1908 and used as an Auxiliary Military Hospital during World War 1, it was then extended in 1925-7 to have 30 beds.

It closed as a hospital in 1979 and is now residential.

Cross Victoria Road and there you will find a grassy area surrounded by 45 Alms Houses and their Chapel (in the North West corner), around Alexandra Square.

Built at Salt's expense for the occupation of the elderly, infirm or destitute, they were furnished, rent free and came with a weekly pension enough to live on, from the mill.

There were many rules. eg 'Not allowed to take in washing' (the pension is enough) and 'Not allowed to leave property for more than 48 hours without permission from mill' (if you are destitute you shouldn't have anywhere to go).

Return back down Victoria Road to the main A657, recross via the zebra crossing and continue down the A657, to the right.

Soon, you meet the junction with Exhibition Road to the left, as shown here.

Turn left down Exhibition Road.

PO16 – The Saltaire Walk

On the right you will see a building belonging to Shipley College.

Opened originally as the Technical School, 30 years after Sir Titus' death, over the door is the inscription 'Created as a memorial to the late Sir Titus Salt Bart'.

Turn left along Mawson Street (or further down Lockwood Street) – both named after the main architects of Saltaire.

Once again we reach Victoria Road and on the other side of the road is another building belonging to Shipley College (of Further Education).

Originally, there were schools, opened 1868, to provide elementary education for 700 boys and girls (one school for boys one for girls).

Later these became Salt's High School for Boys and Girls. Prior to the building of the schools provision was made in the Dining Hall for 'half-timers' education (half a day education, half a day working in the mill).

Note the 'unentitled' Salt coat of arms over the central windows, along with two alpacas, and the initials TS once again over the windows to left and right and in the ironwork of the gate

Points of Interest walks in and around West Yorkshire

Opposite to this building is what is now the Town Hall – but originally was The Institute (built 1867/71).

Here there were classes in art and science, a library, reading room, laboratory, gym, smoking room, billiard room and even a concert hall.

It was home to a choir, gym club, a famous brass band, etc. The architects of the mill, and in fact of the rest of Saltaire, were Mawson and Lockwood. The tower has Salt on all four sides. Above the doorway are the figures of Art and Science and the now official Salt coat of arms (Salt became a baronet in 1869).

If you look at the upper windows you will see that each is surmounted by a carved stone head. All those on the left of the main door are anonymous Romans, but the next two are thought to be the architects Mawson and Lockwood and the final one is of Bacchus (God of wine).

It is commonly thought that Titus was anti-alcohol and so the head of Bacchus is a mystery, but Titus was actually only anti-public houses. He served wine to his guests and didn't object to his tenants keeping beer in their cellars – so he presumably knew of and gave permission for the Bacchus head.

On the doors inside is the Salt motto 'Quid Non Deo Juvante' (Everything is possible with God's help).

It is thought that the four lion statues that surround the Town Hall were originally ordered for Trafalgar Square in London but were rejected as being too small and bought second-hand by Titus for Saltaire.

They represent War, Peace, Vigilance and Determination.

POI6 – The Saltaire Walk

We now return to the car park by continuing down Victoria Road and descend the same stairs we climbed originally – or if using a wheelchair down the road a bit
further and turn right into the yard.

If you are now tempted to visit the mill and view the Hockney exhibition or the antique centre, café, or other facilities, then look for the main entrance near the foot of the stairway, near the corner of the mill (shown here).

If using a wheelchair or if you find stairs difficult but still want to visit, then instead return towards the car park and to the tunnel by the side entrance to the mill as here you will find a lift entry.

I hope that you have enjoyed the walk.

Points of Interest walks in and around West Yorkshire

POI7 – The Holmfirth Walk

The walk is an easy stroll around the area of Holmfirth, West Yorkshire.

It is approximately 1.5 miles but can take up to 1 hour because of all the points of interest to view en route.

It is on hard surfaces and unfortunately, as there are steep steps and slopes, it is not wheelchair friendly.

If you like to feed the ducks then take some food as there is an opportunity right at the start (or end) of the walk.

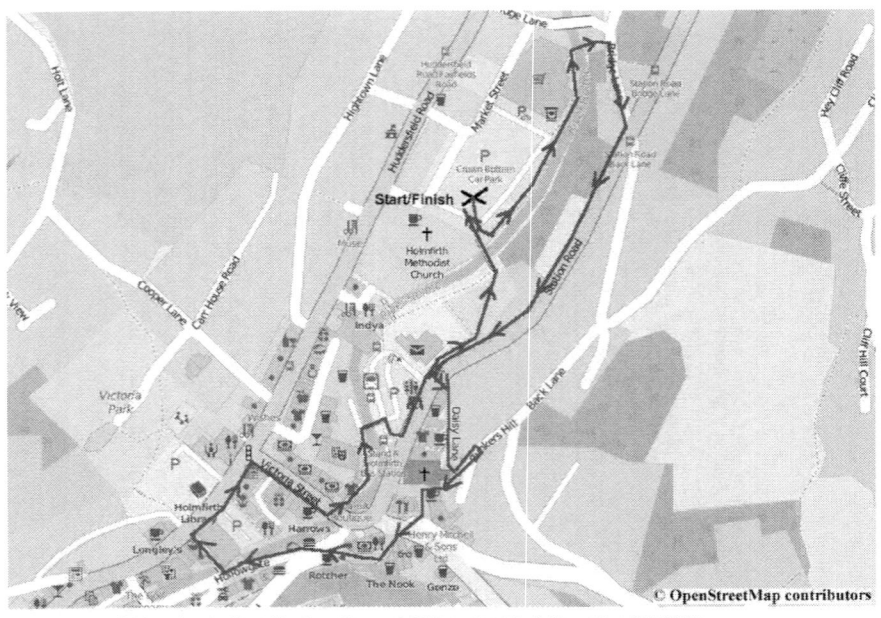

This data is available under the Open Database license and the cartography is licensed as CC BY-SA
Visit http://www.openstreetmap.org/copyright and opendatacommons.org for full copyright details

POI7 – The Holmfirth Walk

START: The walk starts at the Crown Bottom Car Park near the centre of Holmfirth. Set your Sat Nav to HD9 7AX.

The car park is off the main road (Huddersfield Road, A6024) opposite the Town Hall and next to (and forming part of the car park for) the Cooperative Supermarket.

This is a Pay and Display car park – but you can get a refund if shopping in the supermarket.

Leave the car park by the bottom exit furthest from the supermarket (in the corner nearest to the town itself), but do not cross the bridge.

Instead, go down the steps to the riverside and walk left on the path alongside the river.

Here is your opportunity to feed the ducks and, as you can see, there are plenty of them to feed.

Continue walking alongside the river until you come to the bridge, shown here, cross the river via the footbridge and then turn right along Bridge Lane.

Points of Interest walks in and around West Yorkshire

Walk up Bridge Lane until it meets the main road (Station Road) and turn right towards the town centre.

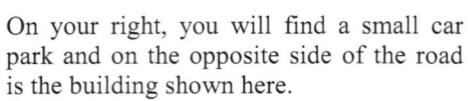

On your right, you will find a small car park and on the opposite side of the road is the building shown here.

This was the Druids Hall, built in 1846 for The Ancient Order of Druids Friendly Society, which had some 600 members in the mid 19th century.

From 1849 to 1860, it served as a chapel for the United Reformed Church.

It was then occupied by the Holmfirth Rifle Volunteers as a drill hall until 1892. Various uses followed, including as a drill hall, a Methodist meeting hall, an early meeting place for Socialists, a hotel and for entertainment.

However, in 1917 the property was acquired and renovated by Holme Valley Masonic Lodge for its own use, which is what it still is today.

POI7 – The Holmfirth Walk

About a hundred metres further down the road, you will see the former warehouse and studio of 'Bamforths & Co, Art Publishers', unfortunately now derelict. James Bamforth set up his photography and painting studio here in 1870 and by 1883 produced lanternslides, which were used in Variety Halls, accompanied by stories and songs, before the invention of cinema.

After cinema was invented, they produced silent comedy films for a number of years until Hollywood took over.

Finally, they became world famous for their production of thousands of saucy seaside postcards (a selection of which are on display in Holmfirth library).

This column is known as Th'owd Genn, possibly after a Wooldale sculptor, Henry Genn.

It was erected in 1801 to celebrate the Peace of Amiens following the war with France that broke out in 1793, although the peace treaty was not finally signed until 1802, the earlier one proving to be just a brief interlude in fighting.

It bears a plaque to show the height of a flood in 1852.

Points of Interest walks in and around West Yorkshire

On February 5th 1852, after heavy rains, the Bilberry Reservoir at Holme Village burst its banks (thought to be due to construction defects) and caused a massive flood, claiming 81 lives, destroying the local Victoria Bridge and immense other damage.

This was a huge event in the history of Holmfirth, taking years from which to recover.

Cross the main road and enter Daisy Lane opposite, as shown here.

Daisy Lane Books in Towngate was once the town Constable's house. The building dates back to 1597 and was once used for collecting taxes, with those who failed to pay up facing a period in the tiny jail further along Towngate on the left.

The Owd Towser, is thought to be the oldest building in Holmfirth (1597).

Originally the church lock-up, over time it has been used as a mortuary, an ambulance station, a jail and a fire station (the basement door is wide enough for the old fire engines).

PO17 – The Holmfirth Walk

Behind the Owd Towser is a path with steps.

Follow this to make a short diversion to pass alongside some cottages called Rattle Row, named from the rattle made by the handlooms that were operated all day long.

At a gap between the cottages, you will find this stone in the opposite retaining wall. These are 'wuzzing holes'.

A woman pushed a pole through a basket, holding wet wool, and with one end supported in one of these holes, spun it round (wuzzed) as a form of 18th Century spin drier.

Walk back down the steps, pass Owd Towser and then continue to the left of the church, down some very steep steps – be very careful and use the handrails.

Within the yard alongside the church is Sid's Cafe, now world famous as the cafe in 'Last of the Summer Wine' TV series and a must-see for most visitors to Holmfirth. It was previously a Fish and Chip shop.

Points of Interest walks in and around West Yorkshire

To the right of the cafe is what was originally the vicarage for the church.

Pass to the left of the cafe and, across the road, you will see the Shoulder of Mutton pub.

On the gable end of the pub is a plaque, celebrating Harold Wagstaff, who captained theEngland Rugby League touring team, in both 1914 and 1920. He was nicknamed 'Prince of Centres'.

Go past the pub along the ginnel shown here.

The ginnel opens up to another pub, previously named the Rose and Crown but renamed as The Nook, as that was how it was known to local people for decades, and now an award winning microbrewery. This is on one of Holmfirth's ancient routes.

POI7 – The Holmfirth Walk

Note its blue plaque that reads:

The Nook. (Previously the Rose and Crown) Established on this site in 1754 and rebuilt in 1819, this inn stands beside the 1768 turnpike route that crosses the adjacent Ribble Beck via 'Higgin Brig'.

The arch of this old bridge can still be seen.

Leave The Nook, crossing over the small bridge (Higgin Brigg), then via another ginnel, as shown here to Hollowgate, where we turn left (along Hollowgate itself).

As you walk along Hollowgate, on the left high on a wall, you will see a blue plaque as shown here.

It commemorates the Beast Market that was held here from the 1900 until 1920.

From 1725 to 1912, the area was used for fairs.

Points of Interest walks in and around West Yorkshire

Further along Hollowgate, opposite a bridge, you will come across the Elephant and Castle pub.

Left of the front door you will find this plaque, which marks the height of a second flood, on 29th May 1944. This was not the result of a reservoir burst – just a cloudburst. It caused a lot of damage again, but luckily this time without any fatalities.

Cross the bridge (Upper Bridge), over the River Holme, directly opposite this pub.

The building on the left, immediately after crossing the bridge, houses another blue plaque.

This is the building that in 1870 replaced what was once the Toll House.

Until 1860, the bridge was part of the main route through the town, after which another bridge was built.

The Toll House was created to collect fees for the Huddersfield to Woodhead Turnpike Trust and also the Greenfield to Shepley Lane Head Turnpike.

PO17 – The Holmfirth Walk

To the left of the Toll House is one of the most famous venues of the Last of the Summer Wine – the cottages of Nora Battye and Compo.

Nora's cottage can be hired as holiday accommodation.

It is possible to mount the steps and walk through, via a ginnel, to the main road – but if you feel uncomfortable then walk back to the Toll House and to the main road that way.

Looking left, you will find the studio/shop of Ashley Jackson, a well-known local artist. (You may know him for his TV programmes, teaching people how to paint.)

Turn to the right along the main road, towards the town centre.

At the main traffic lights turn right down Victoria Street.

At the bottom of Victoria Street, cross the road via the Zebra crossing and go alongside the River Holme, where you will come across the Picturedrome.

Points of Interest walks in and around West Yorkshire

Designed as a cinema, it opened in March 1913 under its original name of the Valley Theatre.

The silent comedy films, made by Balmforth's in the town, were shown. It acted as both a cinema and venue for live concerts as it still does today.

Pass the Picturedrome and cross the River Holme by the footbridge shown here.

Cross the bus station/car park (keep to the right and go straight ahead to the main road) then walk back to the commemorative column that we looked at earlier, Th'owd Genn.
(There are public toilets here if needed.)

Walking away from the column, away from the town centre, and passing the public toilets, you will find an entrance to a small park, which was once a graveyard.

The gravestones are now laid out as a pathway, with others surrounding the park as part of the wall.

Enter the park and cross it diagonally.

POI7 – The Holmfirth Walk

At your exit from the park, you will find yet another commemorative column.

It is the Maythorne Cross.

It is mentioned in 15th century documents and is thought to have been either a boundary marker or the marker of the junction of one of the old salt routes from Cheshire to Yorkshire. The one you see is a replica erected in 2005.

Now cross the bridge in front of you and you are back at the Car Park, where we began. If you didn't feed the ducks at the start of the walk, now you can.

I hope that you enjoyed your walk.

Points of Interest walks in and around West Yorkshire

POI8 – The Harrogate Walk

The walk is an easy stroll around the town of Harrogate, North Yorkshire.

It is approximately 2 miles but can take over 1.5 hours because of all the points of interest to view en route.

It is on hard surfaces and, although there are some steps, these can be avoided and is wheelchair friendly despite some slopes.

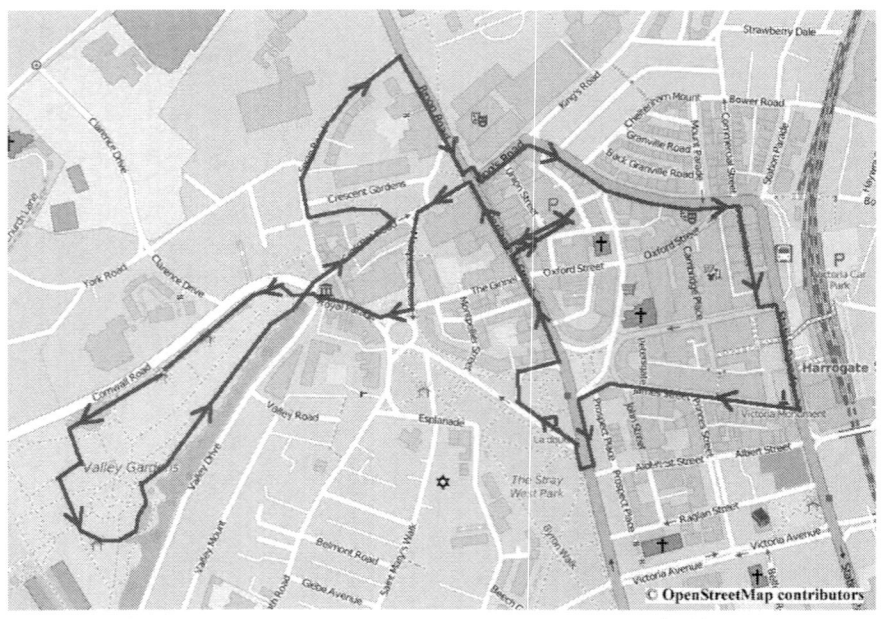

This data is available under the Open Database license and the cartography is licensed as CC BY-SA
Visit http://www.openstreetmap.org/copyright and opendatacommons.org for full copyright details

PO18 – The Harrogate Walk

Harrogate was just a number of small farms until, in 1571, William Slingsby discovered a local spring whose waters were 'beneficial to health'.

From then, visitors flocked to Harrogate to 'take the waters'. The first Pump Room was built in 1786 and its popularity grew and, in Victorian times, many formal buildings were erected; New Victoria Baths (1871), the Royal Baths (1897) and many large hotels.

You can still indulge in a Turkish Bath, massage, or other treatments there today, but nobody 'takes the waters' now, for health and safety reasons. You can still visit the Pump Room museum and smell the water that people drank.

Today, Harrogate still has many grand hotels and hosts large events both inside in the Exhibition Centre and outside, such as the Yorkshire Show and the Flower Show.

START: The walk starts at the multi-storey Jubilee Car Park in the centre of Harrogate. Set your sat nav to HG1 1DJ, and the car park is accessed via Cheltenham Road, from Cheltenham Crescent.

Leave the car park and walk along Union Street in the direction shown here, which is the view you get when leaving the car park.

Turn right at the end of Union Street, downhill to the town, along Oxford Street.

Oxford Street leads to Parliament Street, as shown here, which is one of the main streets of Harrogate.

Cross Parliament Street by the crossing at the end of Oxford Street, as shown, and walk downwards on the left side of Parliament Street.

Points of Interest walks in and around West Yorkshire

On your left you will reach what is now a Wetherspoon's Public House, but, as the arch above the entrance says, was once the 'Winter Gardens', which was part of the Royal Baths. In the 1930s, the Municipal Orchestra played here, in the mornings, every day of the year, with free admission for customers of the Baths.

It was originally a large conservatory-like building with many palms and large plants.

A plaque just outside the entrance reads: 'Wintergarden   Largely inspired by the design of the Crystal Palace, the Wintergarden was built in 1897 for the Royal Baths development. It was largely demolished in 1938 but the original entrance and staircase were preserved.

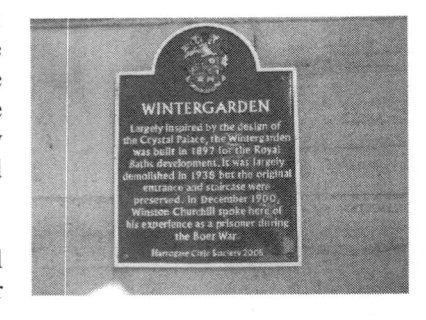

In December 1900 Winston Churchill spoke here of his experience as a prisoner during the Boer War'.

Another plaque on the opposite wall reads: 'Water-Gas Plant   On 2nd August 1890, to the south-east of this plaque, the Mayor of Harrogate, Samson Fox, and inventor of genius, made Parliament Street the world's first route to be lit by his water-gas development. Visitors came from across the UK to see how 'the Mayor of Harrogate has bottled the sun'.

The plant was demolished before the Royal Baths opened in 1897, and following closure in 1969, parts were later acquired for a J D Wetherspoon premises'.

POI8 – The Harrogate Walk

Just beyond the Winter Gardens is the current entrance to the Turkish Baths and spa. You can still take a Turkish Bath or have a massage or other treatment today.

This part of the Royal Baths was completely restored and refurbished in the late 1990s.

Walk further down Parliament Street and turn left at the bottom at the main junction with Crescent Road and here you will find the original entrance to the Royal Baths, now a Chinese Restaurant.

Here you can find this plaque, which reads:

'The Royal Baths were built from 1894-7 by London architects Baggalley and Bristowe, winners of the Harrogate Corporation competition, and opened by H.R.H. The Duke of Cambridge on 23rd July 1897. The sulphur and kissingen springs beneath the building are among the finest in England. The major extension of 1936-9, designed by Leonard Clarke, replaced the Winter Gardens with the Lounge Hall and Fountain Court. The development of the Royal Baths occurred a few years before the building of the Royal Hall and Roundhill Reservoir which together must represent an almost unparalleled example of Municipal Enterprise'.

Points of Interest walks in and around West Yorkshire

Walk past the Royal Baths and the neighbouring Tourist Information Centre and turn left into Montpellier Road as shown here.

You will reach a roundabout.

Keep to the right, passing The Crown hotel, at 300 years old, one of the oldest in Harrogate. Lord Byron, Edward Elgar and even The Beatles, amongst many others, have stayed here.

On your right is The Royal Pump Room, built over the old sulphur well, dating from 1842. Now a museum, you can visit and smell (but not drink) the waters. In 1926, some 1500 glasses of this water were served in one morning.

The motto on the building 'Arx Celebris Fontibus' (also on Harrogate's Coat of Arms) means 'The centre famous for its springs'.

Outside the Royal Pump Room is a free outdoor source of the sulphur water for people to try.

It is guaranteed by an Act of Parliament – but it wasn't working last time I visited.

POI8 – The Harrogate Walk

Directly across the road from the Pump Room is the entrance to Valley Gardens, as shown here.

We will now visit the gardens.

Upon entering Valley Gardens keep to the rightmost path, which will take you into this covered walkway (the Sun Colonnade, 1933).

Walk the whole length of this walkway until it ends and follow the path as shown here and at the nearby junction, just visible here, do not turn left but keep slightly right, but along the path.

At the brow of the path, as it curves left, you will find the New Zealand garden and this Maori Pou Carving.

Here, there are a number of tree sculptures.

Just a little further on the right, you will find the toilets within the park.

Points of Interest walks in and around West Yorkshire

A little further and you find the Pump Room for the Magnesia Well (which is now a cafe and which we will be passing soon on the walk).

Built in 1858, it was recently restored and reopened in October 2015.

Continue past the Pump Room along the path shown here, which curves to the left and takes you downhill to the lower edge of the park.

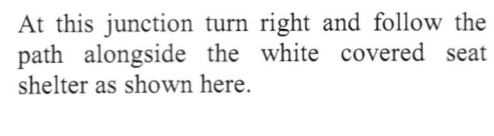

At this junction turn right and follow the path alongside the white covered seat shelter as shown here.

Keep going past the shelter in a straight line as shown in this picture.

POI8 – The Harrogate Walk

This short path leads to the boating lake, which as you see here, on nice sunny days is still used by children with their boats (remote controlled today).

Just past the boating lake you see the Magnesia Well Cafe.

Built in 1895 as the Magnesium Well new pump room.

It is still as popular today as when it was built.

Note the Wishing Well just past the cafe.

On the opposite side of the path is this plaque.

You are now standing in an area known as Bogs Field and the plaque gives information about it, on both sides, including a map of the area.

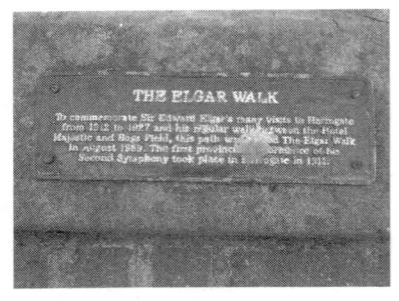

Points of Interest walks in and around West Yorkshire

Carry on down the path to the park entrance where we came in, but along the way, towards the end, note this plaque commemorating the Elgar Walk.

It reads:

'To commemorate Sir Edward Elgar's many visits to Harrogate from 1912 to 1927 and his regular walk between the Hotel Majestic and Bogs Field, the path was called the Elgar Walk in August. The first provincial performance of his Second Symphony took place in Harrogate in 1911'.

Leave the park and walk past Hales Bar (originally the Promenade Inn), the oldest pub in Harrogate which still retains its gas lighting.

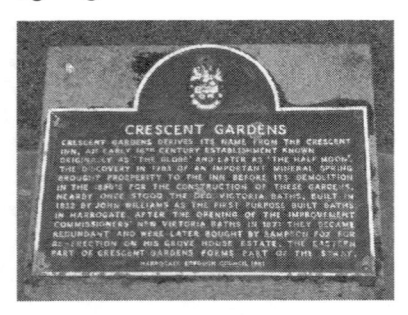

Pass Hales Bar and into Crescent Gardens.

The plaque reads:

'Crescent Gardens derives its name from the Crescent Inn, an early 18th century establishment known originally as The Globe and later as The Half Moon. The discovery in 1783 of an important mineral spring brought prosperity to the inn before its demolition in the 1890s for the construction of these gardens. Nearby once stood the old Victorian Baths, built in 1832 by John Williams as the first purpose built baths in Harrogate, after the opening of the improvement commissioners new Victoria Baths in 1871 they became redundant and were later bought by Sampson Fox for re-erection on his Grove House estate. The eastern part of Crescent Gardens forms part of The Stray'.

POI8 – The Harrogate Walk

This statue of Cupid and Psyche, by Giovanni Maria Benzoni, was placed here in 1862, then later put into storage.

It was restored and re-erected, this time covered to protect it, in 1989.

The council offices were originally the New Victoria Baths.

Always partly used by the council for offices, it was converted to become just offices in the 1930s.

Facing towards the council offices, leave Crescent Gardens uphill, to your left, pavement by the road. There are toilets here too.

At the top of the slope turn, briefly, to your left to view the Mercer Art Gallery, which has free entry and is open most days.

Built in 1805, it was originally Promenade Rooms, as a place for visitors to meet others and as a place to be seen. It has also been used as the Town Hall and as a theatre.

Points of Interest walks in and around West Yorkshire

The plaque on the Art Gallery reads:

'This building was erected in 1805 by private subscription to provide shelter and a meeting place for visitors to the Spa, at a meeting place for visitors to the Spa. At a meeting here on 6th July 1841 the newly formed Harrogate Improvement Commissioners decided to build The Royal Pump Room, remodelled in 1875 by Arthur Hiscoe. The old Town Hall has been variously known as The Promenade Room, The Victoria Room and the Town Hall Theatre. Lily Langtry and Oscar Wilde were two of the many celebrities to appear here'.

Now turn the other way, passing the top of Crescent Gardens once more, walk slightly uphill along Swan Road, passing the Swan Hotel.

It is famous for being the hotel that Agatha Christie was found at after her mysterious disappearance.

To the left of the main door is a plaque, which reads:

'Swan Buildings. Established at the Smiths Arms by 1777, the inn was acquired by Jonathan Shutt in 1782 and renamed The White Swan. After 1848 the Swan, by then a hotel, was owned and enlarged by Isaac Thomas Shutt, architect of the Royal Pump Room. In 1878 Dr Richard Veale converted it into Harrogate's first hydropathic establishment, complete with Turkish Baths, the hotel then becoming known as the Harrogate Hydro. Famous guests included Karl Marx in 1873 and missing novelist Agatha Christie, who was found here in 1926 after the biggest manhunt in British history. Requisitioned in the Second World War for use by the Air Ministry, the hotel re-opened in 1952 as the Old Swan, and was used as a venue for the 1977 film Agatha starring Dustin Hoffman and Vanessa Redgrave'.

POI8 – The Harrogate Walk

Keep going past The Old Swan until Swan Road meets Ripon Road, and turn right, downhill towards the town centre.

Note the huge Majestic Hotel in its own grounds on the opposite side of the road.

On your right, near the bottom of the hill, is the Hotel St George with this plaque:

'Hotel St. George. This hotel grew out of the Chequers Inn built near 18th Century toll bar on the Leeds and Ripon turnpike roads. Renamed The George after George IIIs gift of The Stray in 1778, the hotel was enlarged on several occasions during the 19th century. A fire on 5th May 1927 damaged much of the roof, but the internal stained glass survived. Renamed the St George shortly before the First World War, in the Second World War the hotel was requisitioned by the Post Office and Air Ministry. It reopened in 1952 and acquired a Spa facility in 1985'.

On the opposite side of the road to this hotel is the Royal Hall.

As you can see from the stonework above the main door, this was previously the Kursaal. It changed its name during World War 1 to reflect a more patriotic position.

Opened in 1903 as an entertainment centre for spa visitors, Dame Nellie Melba, Sarah Bernhardt, Lily Langtry and Edward Elgar all appeared here.

Points of Interest walks in and around West Yorkshire

Next door to the Royal Hall is the present Harrogate International Centre, one of Europe's finest conference and exhibition centres with a 2000 seat auditorium and 8 exhibition halls.

Walk past the HIC on your left and along Kings Road until you meet a pedestrian crossing and here cross the road.

Walk uphill, up Cheltenham Crescent.

Near to the top of the road, on your right, you will find Harrogate Theatre.

Cross the road here, and just above Harrogate Theatre walk between all the shops, along Beulah Street, underneath its name arch.

121

POI8 – The Harrogate Walk

At the end of Beulah Street turn left and then right along Station Road (you will see the bus station on the other side of the road) and soon, on your right, you will come across the Victoria Shopping Centre.

Notice, around the roof, the statues that encircle the entire building, not of dignitaries, but of everyday folk of Harrogate.

Further along Station Road is this statue of Queen Victoria.

Turn right at the statue of Victoria, along Victoria Avenue until you come to the end and see the War Memorial, as shown here.

Cross the busy main A61. The best thing is to turn left at the war memorial and walk briefly away from town, where there is a pedestrian crossing. Upon crossing the road, note the grassy areas to the left. This is the beginning of The Stray, a vast 200-acre area of grassland, trees and paths due to the Duchy of Lancaster Commissioners award of 1778 - still free of buildings to this day - and well worth another walk after this one has ended.

Once across the road you will find a modern day commemoration of the Grand Depart of the Tour de France in July 2014.

Points of Interest walks in and around West Yorkshire

At the Tour de France plaque, turn downhill and into a small park, Montpellier Gardens, where you will find this statue, La Douche (the shower).

The plaque that accompanies it reads:

'This statue has been donated to Harrogate by Mrs Frainy Ardeshir in loving memory of her husband's sister Mrs Mehroo Jehangir. Sculpted in France by the notable artist Charles Raphael Peyre, the statue was exhibited at the Paris Salon in 1913 titled La Douche. It was purchased by Sir Dhunjibhoy Bomanji for his principal home, The Willows, in Windsor. It remained in Windsor until the 1950s when Lady Bomanji moved to her Harrogate residence, owned by the family from the mid 1920s. Well known and a generous benefactor to Harrogate, Lady Bomanji was awarded the Freedom of the Borough in 1984. In all her good works she was ably supported by her daughter Mehroo, who continued the family tradition of service and generosity to the town until her own death in 2012'.

From the statue, take the downwards path through the park as shown here.

POI8 – The Harrogate Walk

At the bottom is this carved tree stump, again to commemorate the Grand Depart of the Tour de France July 2014.

One of the buildings to the right, a little further down, was once the Herald Building, where the local newspaper was printed.

On its edifice, high up, you can still make out an advert 'List of Visitors Saturday' and another 'List of Visitors Wednesday'.

This meant that in those papers were printed names of visitors and which hotel they were staying at – so that visitors may know of others here at the same time whom they may wish to visit.

Turn back uphill, through Montpellier Gardens once more, and find this statue to enable you to have your picture postcard photograph taken before you leave.

Points of Interest walks in and around West Yorkshire

Finally, at the top of Montpellier Gardens, you will come across the world famous Betty's Cafe Tea Rooms.

Founded in 1919 by Frederick Belmont, a Swiss confectioner, who married his landlady's daughter when he came to England in 1907. No one knows for sure who Betty was. One theory is that the cafe was named after Betty Lupton, the 'Queen of the Spa' famous for serving spa water for over 60 years. The company says that its favourite story, however, is the one which tells of a small girl interrupting the very first Board Meeting, when the issue of what to call the Tea Rooms was being discussed. The girl's name, of course, was Betty.

From here, either return to The Stray for a longer walk, or progress down Parliament Street, to the next pedestrian crossing, which we crossed at the start of the walk, and return up Oxford Street and then take the first left back to the car park.

I hope that you enjoyed your walk.

POI8 – The Harrogate Walk

Points of Interest walks in and around West Yorkshire

POI9 – The Knaresborough Walk

The walk is an easy stroll around the area of Knaresborough, North Yorkshire.

It is approximately 2 miles but can take over 1.5 hours because of all the points of interest to view en route.

It is on hard surfaces and, although there are some steps, these can be avoided.

It is not really wheelchair friendly, as there are some steep and cobbled slopes, else steps.

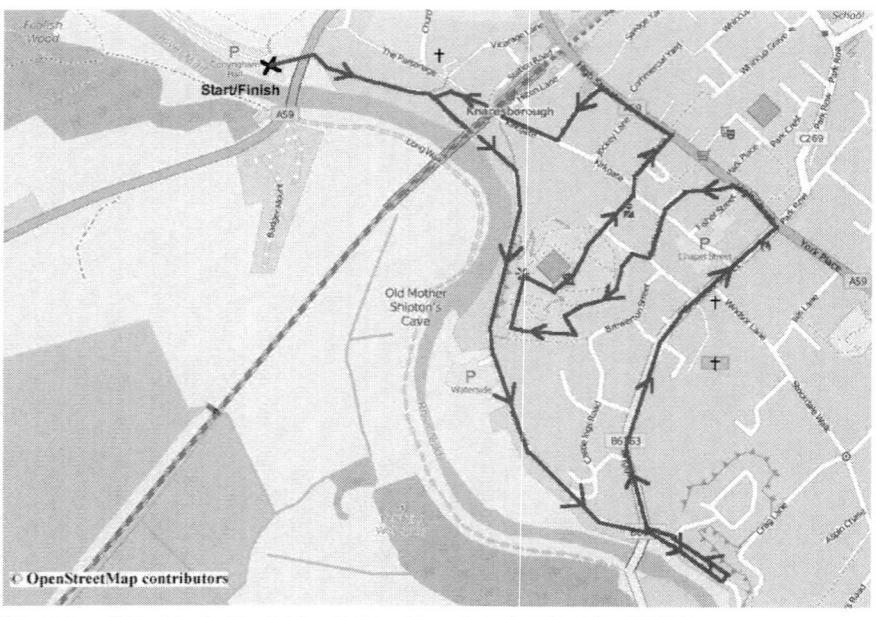

This data is available under the Open Database license and the cartography is licensed as CC BY-SA
Visit http://www.openstreetmap.org/copyright and opendatacommons.org for full copyright details

POI9 – The Knaresborough Walk

Knaresborough was first mentioned in the Domesday Book (1086) and granted to Hugh de Moreville in 1158 (one of the murderers of Thomas Becket) and then to William de Stuteville in 1173.

It has a castle, which overlooks the river Nidd. The castle dates back to the 12th century and, indeed, Hugh de Moreville took refuge there after his involvement in the murder of Becket.

Many changes and modernisations of the castle took place over the next 4 centuries. After the nearby Battle of Marston Moor in 1644, Cromwell ordered the castle to be demolished and hence there is very little left today. What is left is because the local people petitioned parliament to ask for some of it to be left as a prison.

In the late 18th century, a cotton mill was built next to the river, hence the weir, and in the 19th century Knaresborough was famous for its linen production.

START: The walk starts at Conyngham Hall car park, Knaresborough. Set your sat nav to HG5 9AX.

This is a fairly large car park – but is Pay and Display.

The walk should take up to 2 hours but you may want longer as Knaresborough has more to offer.

At the exit to the car park there is a crossing for you to reach the entrance to Waterside as shown here.

Points of Interest walks in and around West Yorkshire

Entering Waterside, you will descend a slope and at the bottom is a Wishing Well to support the local Rotary club. Here is also a small park and in the summer season, there are boats to hire, as shown, and a nice view of the bridge.

This is High Bridge. It has collapsed twice in the past and is famous in that Mother Shipton (1488-1561) prophesied that the world would come to an end when High Bridge collapsed for a third time – hence the name of the pub you have just passed.

Carry along Waterside and, at this junction, keep to the right (keep along Waterside).

Before passing underneath the viaduct, the last building on your right (black and white checks) is the Old Manor House and you will see this plaque which reads:

'This wood frame, grade 2 listed building was built as a hunting lodge for King John. It is believed that following the defeat of the Royalist forces at Marston Moor, articles of capitulation were signed here, in the presence of Oliver Cromwell. A 400 year old mulberry tree planted by James 1st is still fruiting annually in the garden'.

POI9 – The Knaresborough Walk

Pass underneath the viaduct, which carries the railway. It was built between 1846 and 1851.

Nearly completed, it collapsed on 11 March 1848 and took another 3.5 years to rebuild and complete. It is 78ft high above the water and each span is 56ft 9inch across.

Keep on along Waterside until a slight right hand bend in the road, where you will find The Old Dye House on the left as shown.

To the left of the house itself is a plaque.

It reads:

'The Old Dye House. The frontage of the building to your right is all that remains of one of Knaresborough's oldest industrial buildings. Erected in 1610, locally produced textiles were dyed here by John Warner and his son Simon, an active Royalist during the Civil War. The Dye House was an important source of textile dyestuffs supplying the linen mills in the town until 1840'.

To the left of the plaque are Gallons Steps, which lead to Gallon House, near the upper town. Built in the early 19 century consisting of 7 flights of steps, 96 in total, it was named after Richard Nicholas Gallon, who lived in Gallon House.

Points of Interest walks in and around West Yorkshire

Carry on further along Waterside, passing shops and cafes to both left and right, and here again boats can be hired in the summer.

Here you also will find public toilets, next to which are another set of steps up to the upper town, but we will continue along Waterside.

The next building you see on your right alongside the river is Castle Mills. The plaque reads:

'Castle Mills. Built in 1764 Castle Mills is a Grade 2 listed building. From 1770 to 1972 it was a flax mill producing fine quality linen. It was granted the Royal Warrant by Queen Victoria as "Suppliers to all the royal palaces". Closing in 1972 it was converted to 21 dwellings by local builder Ken Hudson'.

At this point Waterside has a junction with Castle Ings Road to the left.

Keep to the right along Waterside.

POI9 – The Knaresborough Walk

You will see a plaque on the wall just before Castle Ings Road - it reads:

'Town Gas Lighting. Knaresborough was one of the first towns to have good street lighting from Sept 1824, thanks to the Improvement Commissioners and their Engineer John Malham. The first gasholder was here at Castle Ings with its Retort House on Waterside but later (2 gasholders) moved across the road. In 1958 there were still 200 gaslights in the town. The last lamplighter retired in 1975 – shortly after the last gasholder was demolished'.

At the end of Waterside, cross the road junction alongside the Half Moon pub and along Abbey Road.

As you enter Abbey Road, passing a small park to the right, look back and note Low Bridge over the Nidd.

Low Bridge is flanked by two pubs: the Mother Shipton Inn and the Half Moon.

Every Boxing Day, the two pubs hold tug of war contests across the river Nidd from this park to the other side.

Carry on further down Abbey Road.

Points of Interest walks in and around West Yorkshire

High on the left is The House in the Rock. Constructed between 1779 and 1791 by Thomas Hill a local linen weaver, it was originally known as Fort Montague. The house has four rooms, one on top of another, and Thomas lived there with his wife and 6 of his 7 children. There is no access now to the House in the Rock as it became a private residence in 2000.

There is a plaque below next to the road.

Go a few yards further down Abbey Road.

Soon you will come across the Chapel of Our Lady of the Crag on the left. It is open (weather permitting) on Sundays between 2.00pm and 4.00pm with extra open days advertised at
www.stmarysknaresborough.org/shrine.html

The plaque reads:

'Chapel of Our Lady of the Crag. In 1408 the Chapel of Our Lady of the The Crag was excavated as a wayside shrine by John the Mason traditionally in thanksgiving for his young son being miraculously saved from a falling rock. Permission for the shrine was granted by King Henry IV'.

POI9 – The Knaresborough Walk

Return now to Low Bridge and turn up the hill away from the river and towards upper Knaresborough, along Briggate as shown here.

Follow Briggate upwards and, on the left, you will encounter Chapel Court, within which is the old Primitive Methodist Chapel, built 1851, but now a private residence. By now Briggate has given way to become Gracious Street.

Further along on the right, just past the George and Dragon pub, you will see these painted windows above two cottages. They are part of a series of such painted images that now embellish buildings in Knaresborough and we will see a number on the walk. The buildings of Knaresborough feature numerous windows, which were blocked up to avoid the window tax, which existed from 1696 to 1851, and gave rise to the expression 'Daylight Robbery'.

The paintings cover these blocked up windows using the technique of trompe l'oeil (to fool the eye) making the images appear real.

They celebrate local people and events and this one is of Guy Fawkes, attempting to blow up parliament in 1605. Fawkes, born in York, lived for many years in Scotton, a village near Knaresborough, where a pub is named after him, and would have visited Knaresborough on numerous occasions.

Points of Interest walks in and around West Yorkshire

Further along on the left, opposite the entrance to Windsor Lane, you can see another example of such blocked up windows.

A little further along Gracious Street, on the left, is the entrance to Chapel Street. Take a short diversion a short way down Chapel Street and back, to view this window painting of John Wesley, on the front of the Methodist Chapel, 1815.

Return to Gracious Street.

Just before the junction of Gracious Street with High Street, on the right, is another of Knaresborough's Town Windows. This one is called Local Hero and represents James 'Ginger' Lacey. Born in Wetherby, he attended King James's School, Knaresborough. He became one of the best-known fighter pilots of World War 2, shooting down 28 planes in total (18 during the Battle of Britain).

Turn left at the junction of Gracious Street and High Street, pass the Board Inn. You will pass the area set aside for local buses on the left and on the right is another of the Town Windows. This one commemorates the now closed Knaresborough zoo, which thrived from 1965 to 1985 in the grounds of Conyngham Hall, near our starting point at the car park.

135

POI9 – The Knaresborough Walk

Just past this Window, leave the High Street, go down Silver Street towards the Market Place, which upon arriving we will investigate and return to Castlegate (the street to your left as you enter and via which we will leave).

The Market Cross. The base dates back to 1709, when a previous cross was erected, but in 1824 the cross was replaced by a gas lamp, later to become an electric lamp.

No market should be without a Cross and so the current one was built to celebrate the Queen's Coronation in 1953 and is designed in the style of a 14th century cross.

We pass a statue to Blind Jack (1717-1810) sitting with an instrument (a surveyor's wheel) for measuring road distances.

He was famous as a road builder, despite being totally blind from the age of 6, following smallpox.

Following an act of Parliament in 1765, new roads were to be built and Blind Jack (John Metcalf) built a section of the road between Knaresborough and Harrogate.

So successful was he that he became one of the best road builders, finally being responsible for nearly 180 miles of road.

Points of Interest walks in and around West Yorkshire

This Window in the Market Place also celebrates Blind Jack, but this time his earlier life. He learnt to play the fiddle and, aged 15, became fiddler at the Queen's Head in High Harrogate.

He later earned money as a guide (especially at night) and one day eloped with the daughter of the landlord of the Royal Oak in Harrogate (later the Granby).

He even marched to Scotland to join the army fighting Bonnie Prince Charlie's rebels – not as a soldier, but moving guns over boggy ground.

This was the oldest pharmacy shop in England. Ye Olde Chymist Shoppe dispensed medicines continuously from 1720 until 1997.

It bears its own blue plaque next to the front door. It is now a cafe and sweet shop.

Leave the Market Square by Castlegate (near to where you entered) as shown here.

On the Market Tavern, Castlegate, is this painting of Mother Shipton, who is probably Britain's best-known witch. Once you finish the walk you are invited to visit the 'Dropping Well' and hear the full story of Mother Shipton, via a walk on the other side of the river (charges apply) by crossing High Bridge near the car park.

POI9 – The Knaresborough Walk

Past the Market Tavern, you will come across Green Dragon Yard on your left.

Here was The Old Flax Mill where, from the 19th century, raw flax or linen, was combed in preparation for spinning or weaving. It is now home to the Art in the Mill gallery.

Just past Green Dragon Yard, on the left, you will see another two Town Windows one on top of the other, showing the artist herself in two self-portraits, doing the work, (not shown here).

On the right, a little further down Castlegate is this Window showing King John. Despite his poor reputation (Robin Hood) he strengthened Knaresborough castle and used it as a base for hunting. The first known Royal Maundy service took place in Knaresborough when, in 1210, he gave money to 13 poor men as shown in the painting.

At the end of Castlegate turn right along Castle Yard.

Walk to the castle entrance to your left, as shown here and into the grounds of Knaresborough Castle.

Points of Interest walks in and around West Yorkshire

Once through the gates take the path to your left.

Just as you enter the castle, along this path, to the right you will see the Sallyport. It is worth taking a look at the Sallyport if the ground isn't too wet to get to it. A Sallyport is a tunnel large enough for a small group of armed men to leave the castle and attack any besieging troops. There are two such for this castle but only one has been excavated. They were built in the late 13th or mid 14th centuries.

Keep walking along the path around the castle grounds and you will come across the bowling green and, set back, The Courthouse Museum. Some parts of the Courthouse date back to the 12th or 13th century with additions in the 16th century. It is open daily from 11am to 4pm during the spring/summer period.

Keep on the same path until you come to Knaresborough War Memorial, with 156 names from World War 1 and 55 from World War 2 of soldiers from Knaresborough who lost their lives.

PO19 – The Knaresborough Walk

Look over the wall near the War Memorial and this view shows the weirs that served the linen mill to the left, which we passed earlier on the walk, now converted to dwellings – Castle Mills.

Further along the path is another part of the castle museum, open daily from Easter to September 11am-4pm. When open, visitors can also enjoy crown green bowling and putting and can hire the equipment from the museum.

To the left of the castle is the most famous view of Knaresborough, back to the viaduct and the river Nidd.

Keep walking past the castle and leave the grounds by the gateway shown here (not the same one you came in by).

Upon leaving the castle ground, keep going straight ahead, winding your way through a small car park with the Police Station ahead on your right.

On the left is the old Dispensary as shown here. It was erected in memory of a late vicar the Rev A Cheap LLB 1853.

Points of Interest walks in and around West Yorkshire

Turn left at the Castle Vaults pub.

Here is a restaurant called Six Poor Folk – relating to its use in the 17th century as a hospital for six poor folk.

This blue plaque on The Six Poor Folk reads:

'Knaresborough Almshouse. The mouldings and roof structure of these buildings indicate a probable date before 1500, and perhaps around 1450. Originally one large and impressive building, it was listed in the Survey of 1611 as a hospital for six poor folk'.

Across the road from the Six Poor Folk, you will see this Town Window. This painting is of is Queen Philippa, wife of Edward III, and he gave her Knaresborough Castle as part of her marriage settlement. She lived there occasionally from 1332. The picture shows her giving a casket of money to restore the Parish Church, which she did.

Keep walking away from the castle, but not down Kirkgate, and just beyond the above Window, we are on one side of Market Square, where this is another blue plaque. This one is on the outside of what is now the Library and Customer Service Centre. It celebrates the original location of the Knaresborough Synagogue.

141

POI9 – The Knaresborough Walk

It reads: 'In the 13th century a Jewish community lived and worshipped in Knaresborough. The Synagogue was situated at the exit to Synagogue Lane, at the rear of these buildings, the exact location is unknown. It is believed the Knaresborough Jewish community was dissolved in 1275, before all of the Jewish faith were expelled from England in 1290'.

Keep going in this direction past Market Square to the High Street and turn left. After a hundred yards or so on High Street, you will see the building shown here. It is called Cromwell House. Cromwell stayed here for 2 nights in 1648, during the demolition of the castle, although the building is much altered since.

The room he used is above the arch and, despite all the alterations, the floor of that room was left untouched.

Turn left off the High Street, directly opposite Cromwell House, down Finkle Street.

Note the ginnels on the right as you walk down Finkle Street until it meets Kirkgate and turn right at that junction.

Walk down Kirkgate and on the left you will find Gallons House as shown here.

To its right is an opening with steps down – these are the Gallons Steps that we saw earlier when passing along Waterside.

Points of Interest walks in and around West Yorkshire

At this point we meet the railway line that passes over the viaduct and we need to cross to the other side – to the right-hand side is an underpass – it is recommended to take that and be safe.

On the other side of the railway, keep walking until you meet Water Bag Bank on your left as shown here. Take this cobbled path down to Waterside, and take care as it is steep and could be slippery if wet.

Until the 19th century, the town used water from the river, which was brought up via this street using leather bags, carried either by donkey or even by hand (women carried the water for halfpenny a time). This was not the only source of water for the town.

At the bottom of Water Bag Bank we return to Waterside that we walked along earlier. Turn right and follow Waterside to return to the car park. If you have the time and energy you may, instead, cross High Bridge and walk down the other side of the river to see the Dropping Well and the history of Mother Shipton – there is a charge for entry.

I hope that you enjoyed your walk.

POI9 – The Knaresborough Walk

Points of Interest walks in and around West Yorkshire

POI10 – The Otley Walk

The walk is an easy stroll around the town of Otley, North Yorkshire.

It is approximately 1.5 miles but can take over 1 hour because of all the points of interest to view en route. It is on hard surfaces and is wheelchair friendly.

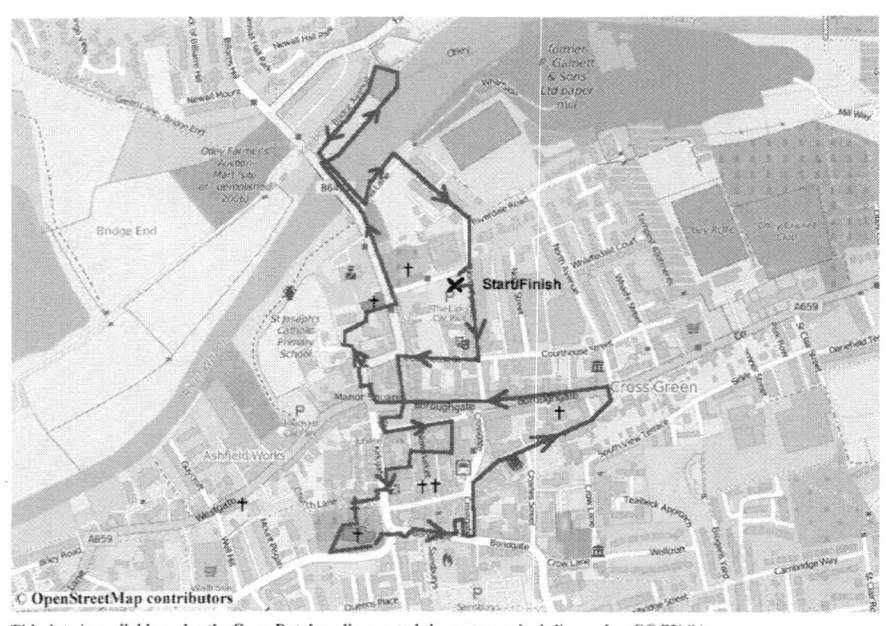

This data is available under the Open Database license and the cartography is licensed as CC BY-SA
Visit http://www.openstreetmap.org/copyright and opendatacommons.org for full copyright details

The name Otley is of Saxon origin from Othe, Otta or Otho, a Saxon personal name, and leah, a woodland clearing in old English – hence the Saxon cross relics in the Parish church, which you may see on your walk. The town proper began in the 13th century with markets granted Royal Charter in 1222 by Henry III. There were worsted mills during the Industrial revolution, but by 1900 over 2000 people were employed locally in the printing machinery trade, following the invention of the Wharfedale Printing Machine in Otley. A large paper mill next to the river was also a big employer for 150 years but now sadly has been demolished. Probably the best-known person to come from Otley is Thomas Chippendale the 18th century cabinetmaker.

POI10 – The Otley Walk

START: The walk starts at one of Otley's main car parks (Licks Car Park), in the centre of the town, as shown here.

Set your Sat Nav to LS21 1BA. It is a Pay and Display car park so make sure that you display a ticket.

Previously the site of the Licks Cattle Market, the cattle market was moved here from Manor Square in 1885. The Licks also became the site for the Bank Holiday feast and fair.

Leave the car park by the North Parade exit and walk down North Parade towards the town centre, as shown here.

Turn right at the first junction on the right, into Courthouse Street, as shown.

The Courthouse is now used as a Community performance and arts outreach centre, with a café, offering regular activities for young people. Feel free to look in if it is open. The original building dates from 1856 but has been changed dramatically since then. In its time, it has been a Fire Station, Police Headquarters, a cellblock for prisoners and then a magistrate's court, ceasing to be a court in 1997.

Points of Interest walks in and around West Yorkshire

Continue to the end of Courthouse Street to its junction with Bridge Street, as shown here.

Look to the other side of Bridge Street, where you will see a building currently housing a firm of solicitors, but earlier it was once the Royal Oak public house. You will see a stone above one doorway dating the building to 1651 and above the other doorway a wonderfully stone-carved name stone with oak branches too.

On your left, opposite the Royal Oak is the ginnel shown here. Enter the ginnel, it will take you to the Market Square.

Walk all the way through, exiting Bay Horse Court via another ginnel and into the light of Boroughgate, next to the Market Square.

Cross Boroughgate and enter Market Square and follow the path shown here to the Clock.

If it is a Tuesday, Friday or Saturday the square will be full

POI10 – The Otley Walk

The Clock was built in 1887 to celebrate Queen Victoria's Golden Jubilee.

However three other events are commemorated here too, now.

The earliest addition is a plaque to two local soldiers, Trooper John Wilton Sedman and Sapper John Ventriss Duell, who died during the Transvaal War 1899-1902.

Next is a stone presented in 1915 by grateful Belgian refugees, who came to Otley when World War I broke out, to show their appreciation for the help given by the folk of Otley.

Finally, there is a plaque to commemorate Victory in Europe and Victory in Japan in 1945 at the end of World War II.

Also, note the tiny door into the tower.

The Buttercross. It is possibly Otley's oldest building, but has been rebuilt many times since its construction in medieval times. Originally used to sell dairy produce plus rabbits, ducks, etc, it is now somewhere sheltered to sit, or can be hired, free of charge from the local council for charity stalls.

Points of Interest walks in and around West Yorkshire

On the opposite side of the road to the Market Clock you will see The Old Hall, Kirkgate, shown here. Built around 1700, it was once the family home of Mr Thomas Lacon Barker (1717-1773).

The ground floor was converted to shops in the early 1840s.

Walk back into the Market Square and walk past The Black Bull.

Note the plaque on the wall of The Black Bull – it tells it all.

Keep going down this pavement until you meet the entrance to Orchard Gate, shown here. You now enter a rabbit warren of little streets and shops, some new buildings, some old. Please spend some time exploring this small area of the town.

Keeping to the right, eventually you need to find the entrance to New Inn Court as shown here. Go into this ginnel and work your way through to the far exit, back to Kirkgate (the street where the Clock and the Old Hall were).

You will emerge opposite the Red Lion pub.

POI10 – The Otley Walk

Turn left along Kirkgate and cross the road via the crossing to reach Kirkgate Arcade. Note the Art Nouveau balustrade above the entrance and the clock, which reads 'Never Give Up' on its face.

You may care to look into the arcade, which has a number of interesting shops and some lovely chandeliers.

Now enter the lane to the left of Kirkgate Arcade, just before the entrance to the churchyard.

Behind some railings on your right you will see the Navvies Monument shown here. Over 2,000 men worked on the Bramhope Tunnel, which is over 2 miles long, constructed between 1846 and 1849.

23 men lost their lives during the work and the memorial is a replica of the north portal and records the names of those 23 navvies.

Just above the Navvies Monument, you enter the churchyard via this small gate.

Feel free to look into the church, which is open for visitors Monday – Friday 9am-5pm and Saturday morning. The first church built on this site, is thought to have been in 627AD and some of the current building is Norman. The church houses relics of Saxon Runic crosses over 1300 years old.

Points of Interest walks in and around West Yorkshire

You must now return to Kirkgate. If using a wheelchair, the best advice would be to retrace your steps and then turn right on Kirkgate (away from the Arcade) to the road junction. Otherwise, you may continue around the churchyard path to the same spot, where there are steps at the end down to Kirkgate.

We now walk down Bondgate.

Here, Dowgill House has a datestone of 1753 and Chippendales Tea Rooms has a notice that Thomas Chippendale lived there.

The row of flagstones outside the cafe marks the now underground route of Cale Head Beck.

Cross Bondgate to the Bowling Green pub. The plaque to the left of the front door reads: 'This Grade II listed building was erected 1757 by Nathaniel Aked, hence the letters NA above the datestone on the west end. The bricked up doorway under the datestone was once reached by an outside staircase. The upper storey was used as the town's assembly rooms and later as a place of worship. The Bowling Green Inn took over the whole of the building in 1825. The premises were refurbished by J D Wetherspoon in June 2010'.

A second plaque on the building, to the right of the front door, reads 'Built 1767 formerly a Chapel, School, Courthouse and Assembly rooms, becoming an Inn during 1865' - so the two plaques contradict each other – who do you believe Otley Town Council or J D Wetherspoon?

POI10 – The Otley Walk

A few yards further down Bondgate are the Memorial Gardens.

This hosts a replica Saxon cross, being a full sized replica of one of the cross remnants that are housed in the Parish Church, which you may have seen earlier.

The Memorial Gardens are at the junction of Bondgate and Crossgate and, at this junction, we find the Rose and Crown public house as shown. You will notice to its left are two gates to the rear of the pub.

Cross the road and, if the gates are open, enter the rear yard.

Hopefully, the yard is open and here you will find this metal cross embedded in the wall to the left of the yard (not the wall of the pub).

It is known as a Corn Cross, but little is known about it.

Walk down Crossgate until you meet Nelson Street and progress to the right along Nelson Street.

Points of Interest walks in and around West Yorkshire

Nelson Street soon becomes Walkergate.

Keep going until Walkergate opens up to become Manchester Square as shown here.

Here you find not one but two Maypoles. The very tall one is some 75 feet tall and is the tallest Maypole in Britain.

A maypole has stood here for over 200 years. The current one is a very recent version from (2014). The previous one was condemned for health and safety when Otley was part of the route of the famous Tour de France cycle race. The smaller one is the only one actually used for Mayday dances nowadays.

In Manchester Square, you will find the building shown here. Originally, the Mechanics Institute, latterly the Civic Centre, it has now fallen into disuse.

The road back into Otley centre is called Boroughgate. Leave Manchester Square by crossing Boroughgate and walking left towards the town centre, on the right-hand side of the road.

After crossing a road to your right, where there are traffic lights (this is North Parade that leads back to the car park), you will see on the next building this plaque, which celebrates the birth of Thomas Chippendale at this spot in a cottage that once stood here.

POI10 – The Otley Walk

Before you reach the Bay Horse pub, you will find a cottage with this plaque showing that not only did a Dr John Ritchie live there but also John Wesley stayed here often.

Look for the plaque shown here, on the Bay Horse pub, which lists a history of Otley. Note the earliest reference is to the Saxon cross from the church, a replica of which we also saw (it is dated here as of 750AD).

Outside the Bay Horse public house are 3 benches, each of which bears a different poetic notice to make you smile.

The Black Horse Hotel is at the end of Boroughgate. Note the superb architectural detail. The original building dated from 1821 but was demolished in 1900 and the current one was completed a year later.

Turn right at the end of Boroughgate into Manor Square and cross the road by the pedestrian crossing shown here.

Points of Interest walks in and around West Yorkshire

Walk around Manor Square until you come to the statue of Thomas Chippendale, famous for his furniture designs in the 18th Century.

The building behind the statue is the Old Grammar School and the current use is now as an art gallery.

Walk alongside the statue of Chippendale and soon you will see the building shown here.

This is the Manor House, built in 1792 within the grounds of the medieval Palace of the Archbishop of York, but not on the same spot.

Indeed, the original site intended for this house was further along the river but, whilst the person for whom it was built, a Mr Wilson, was away on business, his wife had the pegs removed, the foundations laid here instead and building work well underway by his return, as she wanted a view down Kirkgate.

The plaque on the Manor House gives its date and shows that it is within the grounds of an original Episcopal Manor House.

Keep going and leave the Manor House via the side of the church to meet Bridge Street as shown here.

Cross Bridge Street and then turn left, away from the town centre.

POI10 – The Otley Walk

As the name of the street suggested, you will come across Otley Bridge, which we will now cross.

Built in 1675 replacing a previous one destroyed by a flood, it crosses the river at its widest point and was itself widened in 1776.

Once across the bridge there are some steps down into the park – Wharfedale Meadows.

If you are a wheelchair user continue a few yards further past the steps where a second entrance to the park is level.

This sculpture, commissioned to celebrate the Queen's Diamond Jubilee, is a celebration of both the importance of printing and paper to Otley and the continued importance of education to the town. David Payne invented the Wharfedale Printing Machine, whilst working for William Dawson of Otley, who manufactured these machines and it was state of the art in its day.

Further down the park we will meet a large weir that was needed by a huge paper mill on the other side of the river, now sadly demolished.

Unveiled in 1993, this spectacular sundial commemorates

'Sam Hartley Chippindale 1909-1990, born in Otley, Property and Shopping Centre developer – Public benefactor PIONEER, GENIUS AND LEGEND'.

Points of Interest walks in and around West Yorkshire

Walk in the park until you meet the weir – worth it for the sound alone. This served the factory of P Garnett & Sons, which made paper on the other side of the river for 150 years until it stopped production in 2005 and was demolished in favour of a new housing estate.

Turn left alongside this building (there are toilets here if need be) and turn left again at the end as we intend to return now and leave the park. However, the path alongside the river, and the park itself, continue much further and so if you wish, please continue to explore but return to this point to exit the park.

Return to the bridge, with the cottages on your right.

Recross the bridge and immediately turn left along Mill Lane. Unfortunately, at the time of writing your path is soon blocked by development work, but at the first opportunity we will turn right anyway to return to the car park.

Walk up Manor Street and you will soon find yourself back at your car park.

I hope that you enjoyed the walk.